CORNISH COASTAL WALKS
FOR MOTORISTS

Warne Gerrard Guides for Walkers

Walks for Motorists Series

CHESHIRE WALKS
CHILTERNS WALKS
       Northern
       Southern
CORNISH COASTAL WALKS
COTSWOLD WALKS
       Northern
       Southern
COUNTY OF AVON WALKS
COUNTY OF DURHAM WALKS
DARTMOOR WALKS
DERBYSHIRE WALKS
       Northern
       Southern
DORSET WALKS
ESSEX WALKS
EXMOOR WALKS
FAMILY WALKS IN MIDLAND COUNTIES
FURTHER CHESHIRE WALKS
FURTHER DALES WALKS
GREEN LONDON WALKS (both circular and cross country)
HAMPSHIRE AND THE NEW FOREST WALKS
HEREFORD AND THE CENTRAL WELSH BORDERS WALKS
HERTFORDSHIRE WALKS
ISLE OF WIGHT WALKS
JERSEY WALKS
KENT WALKS
LAKE DISTRICT WALKS
       Central
       Northern
       Western
LOTHIAN AND SOUTH EAST BORDERS WALKS
MIDLAND WALKS
NORTHUMBERLAND WALKS
NORTH YORK MOORS WALKS
       North and East
       West and South
PEAK DISTRICT WALKS
PENDLESIDE AND BRONTE COUNTRY WALKS
SEVERN VALLEY WALKS
SNOWDONIA WALKS Northern
SOUTH DEVON WALKS
SOUTH DOWNS WALKS
SURREY WALKS
WYE VALLEY WALKS
YORKSHIRE DALES WALKS

Long Distance and Cross Country Walks

RAMBLES IN THE DALES
WALKING THE PENNINE WAY
NORTH TO SOUTH ALONG THE PENNINE WAY

Warne Gerrard Guides for Walkers

CORNISH COASTAL

WALKS FOR MOTORISTS

Eleanor Smith

**30 circular walks with sketch maps
by F. Rodney Fraser**

FREDERICK WARNE

Published by
Frederick Warne (Publishers) Ltd
40 Bedford Square
London WC1B 3HE

Acknowledgement

My thanks go to my family for their help in this project, particularly to my husband Joe and sons Andrew and David.

Publishers' Note

While every care has been taken in the compilation of this book, the publishers cannot accept responsibility for any inaccuracies. Things may have changed since the book was published; paths are sometimes diverted, a concrete bridge may replace a wooden one, stiles disappear. Please let the publishers know if you discover anything like this on your way.

The length of each walk in this book is given in miles and kilometres, but within the text Imperial measurements are quoted. It is useful to bear the following approximations in mind: 5 miles = 8 kilometres, ½ mile = 805 metres, 1 metre = 39.4 inches.

ISBN 0 7232 2814 0

Phototypeset, printed and bound by Galava Printing Co. Ltd., Nelson, Lancashire

Contents

			Page
Introduction			7
North coast walks			
Walk	1	Boscastle	10
	2	Nectan's Glen	13
	3	Tintagel	16
	4	Daymer Bay	19
	5	Newquay and Watergate Bay	21
	6	Newquay and East Pentire	23
	7	Crantock	26
	8	Perranporth	28
	9	Chapel Porth	30
	10	Portreath	32
	11	St Ives	34
	12	Levant	36
	13	St Just	38
	14	Sennen Cove and Land's End	40
South coast walks			
	15	Lamorna	42
	16	Mousehole	44
	17	St Michael's Mount	46
	18	Penrose Woods	48
	19	Lizard Head	50
	20	Kennack Sands	52
	21	Helford	55
	22	Anthony Head	57
	23	Restronguet Creek	60
	24	Coombe Creek	62
	25	Mevagissey	64
	26	Fowey	67
	27	Polkerris	70
Moorland walks			
	28	Cheesewring, Bodmin Moor	72
	29	Bodmin Moor, Brown Willy and Rough Tor	74
	30	Madron Moor	76

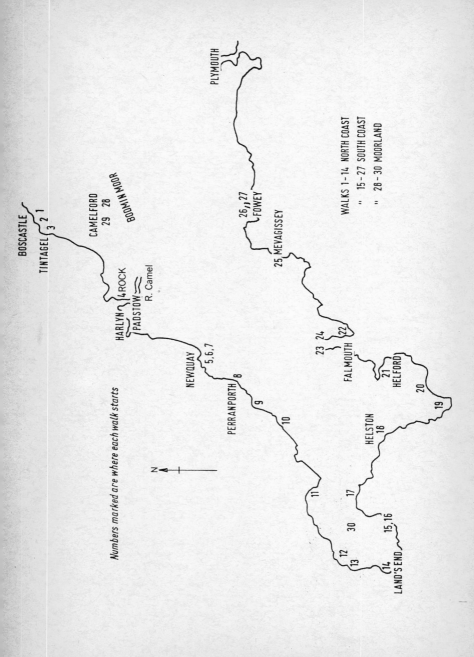

BOSCASTLE

TINTAGEL 2 1
3

CAMELFORD
29 28
BODMIN MOOR

HARLYN 4 ROCK
PADSTOW
R. Camel

NEWQUAY
5, 6, 7

PERRANPORTH 8

9

10

11

12
13
14
LAND'S END
15,16

30

17

HELSTON
16

FALMOUTH
23 24 22

HELFORD
21
20
19

MEVAGISSEY
25

26,,27
FOWEY

PLYMOUTH

WALKS 1 - 14 NORTH COAST
"   15 - 27 SOUTH COAST
"   28 - 30 MOORLAND

Numbers marked are where each walk starts

N

Introduction

Cornwall, a county almost surrounded by water, must offer some of the best coastal walking in the country. The river Tamar rises four miles inland from Marsland Mouth on the North coast and flows south to reach the sea at Plymouth forming the boundary of Devon and Cornwall. The Atlantic Ocean rolls in to the North coast and the English Channel to the south.

The geology of Cornwall makes this a county of vast contrasts. The country rock of slate has been intruded by the granites of Bodmin, Carnmenellis and Madron Moors, while the serpentine rock which forms the Lizard area has a long history and may have been formed beneath an ocean, millions of years ago. Geologists find the county forever interesting with its complex rock formations. The china clay district of St Austell consists of decomposed granite forming the mineral kaolin. This valuable commodity, used in so many items of daily life from paint to medicines, is the backbone of Cornish industry today. The intrusion of the granites caused the mineralisation of these areas which, from prehistoric times, have occasioned the rise and fall of the fortunes of this unique county.

Mineral extraction, today, consists of tin being mined at South Crofty, Wheal Jane and Mount Wellington in the Redruth area and Geevor mine in the West Penwith area. Further drilling operations are taking place on Redmoor near Callington. In the years between the fifteenth and nineteenth centuries, hundreds of small mines were operating, producing vast quantities of tin, copper, lead and associated minerals. The collapse of this industry came with the discovery of alluvial deposits in the Far East which could be extracted more cheaply.

Immense fortunes were amassed by the mineral lords during the heyday of Cornish mining and the reminders of past glories are with us today in the properties and possessions of these people, now often in the care of the National Trust. Coastal walking in Cornwall will bring this part of history to mind as small ports and harbours, built to bring in the coal and export the ore, are visited during the walks. Tall chimneys of the engine houses with their associated derelict buildings, often covered with ivy and brambles, have a strange beauty which has inspired many artists to put brush to canvas.

Cornwall also had its fishing heyday. Vast shoals of pilchards, numbered in millions, approached the coasts during the late summer, August to October. These were sighted from look-out posts known as 'Huer's Huts'. When the shout went up that the shoal had been seen the fishermen would take to their boats and surround the fish with a seine net. Once hauled to the beach the women and children played their part in helping to unload and cure the fish which were placed in barrels and exported to Latin countries to be eaten during Lent. The local toast was often given as 'Copper, tin, fish and the Pope'. The pilchards, following the movement of their food, largely ceased to approach these shores about a hundred years ago and only very limited numbers are caught today.

Cornwall's prehistory offers the archaeologist a wealth of interesting material. There are the passage graves, entrance graves, quoits or dolmans, standing stones and stone circles. The Romano-British village of Chycauster, near Penzance, now in the care of the Department of the Environment, is known to be one of the best preserved of its kind in the country. The hill and promontory forts are well defined and holy wells have their place in many villages.

The only city in Cornwall is Truro and this offers the visitor a first class museum, a lovely cathedral and interesting old buildings and streets. The Truro river, a tributary of the Fal, flows through the city and boats are still to be seen moored at Lemon Quay. Truro is fast becoming the administration centre of Cornwall in place of Bodmin. Geographically more central, it affords better facilities for government departments. The courts, however, still hold their sittings at Bodmin which keeps its status as the County Town.

Cornwall, today, is essentially a county of tourism with its mild climate, beautiful beaches, spectacular coastline and dominating moors. Who can but call it a 'Delectable Duchy'? Many of the tourist-related businesses are owned by people from the North, the Midlands and London most of whom have integrated well with local society.

I am an inveterate coastal walker, be it wet and windy or calm and sunny. I never tire of the same walk as each season offers its own variations and the sea is forever changing. I hope that you who use these walks will feel that Cornwall can still be a place in which to 'get away from it all'. Your car can take you so far but the true beauty-spots can only be found by walking to discover the coasts of Cornwall.

Cliff paths

All the walks described here are on official rights of way. Cliff paths are subject to erosion and detours may have to be made, particularly after a stormy winter. Much of the coastline comes under the care of the National Trust or the Countryside Commission and is usually well-signposted. It is never wise to walk the coastal footpath during a gale. Strong winds can make walking a real hazard and gusts of up to 100 mph have been recorded.

Beaches

Vast stretches of golden sands and sheer cliffs are beautiful to look at, but the walker must watch for a fast incoming tide. It cannot be stressed too strongly that one never walks round a jutting headland at beach level on a rising tide. Plan your walk around the tide chart, readily and cheaply available at most newsagents.

Equipment

Good, stout, waterproof boots and thick socks are advisable, both for comfort and to help to avoid the twisted ankles that can occur, particularly when walking with inadequate footwear over wet rocks. A good waterproof is another necessity since storms from the Atlantic blow up very suddenly. Although the sketch maps in this book should be sufficient, the relevant 1:50,000 Ordnance Survey sheet number is given at the beginning of each walk as well as the name of the nearest town used as a starting point.

General

The walks in this book are suitable for the average person who likes a moderate ramble. Yet cliff paths can be steep and, while attention has been given to avoiding the worst of these, some of the lesser ones are included where places of special interest are involved. A note is made of this before any walk incorporating any steep ascent or descent. Children over the age of eight should be able to cope with most of the walks and parents prepared to carry a young one in a papoose type sling should manage very well. I would not feel it advisable to take a toddler or a pushchair on any coastal walk given here.

The Country Code, which must be observed at all times, is as follows:

Enjoy the countryside and respect its life and work
Guard against all risk of fire
Fasten all gates
Keep your dogs under close control
Keep to public paths across farmland
Use gates and stiles to cross fences, hedges and walls
Leave livestock, crops and machinery alone
Take your litter home
Help to keep all water clean
Protect wildlife, plants and trees
Take special care on country roads
Make no unnecessary noise.

With this in mind, do take your time, your camera and binoculars and enjoy all that Nature has to offer in this lovely county of Cornwall.

Walk 1   Boscastle Harbour, Church and Village

4 miles (6.5 km)

OS sheet 190

Boscastle harbour and village, nestling at the foot of some of the highest and most spectacular cliffs in Cornwall, are now a sleepy holiday area, very different from the bustling places they must have been until the early years of this century. From here the slate extracted from the Delabole Slate Quarry was exported. This quarry still exists today and the large hole in the ground, one mile in circumference, is evidence that for the past 700 years this industry has been operating. There were boat yards, sail lofts and a forge in the harbour area but they are now a Youth Hostel, gift shop and café. It is here that the river Valency crossed by a new bridge — the old one having been swept away in floods in 1957 — makes its way down to the sea.

The nearest town to Boscastle is Camelford and it is from here that our route is taken. Leave Camelford by the B3266, following the signposts to Boscastle. This road enters the village down a very steep hill and the panorama before your eyes on turning a sharp bend is quite breathtaking. There is a National Trust car park on the harbour or a council one just over the bridge. Before starting the walk take a look at the water-wheel working away as of old beside the mill which is now a craft area where interesting and unusual examples of work may be seen.

The walk starts along the harbour, keeping to the left side. Carefully pass the bollards and mooring ropes and come on to the ancient jetty, built in 1584. Nearly opposite the jetty is the outer bar, originally built in the late 1700's but blown up by a World War II mine and rebuilt by the National Trust in 1962. Look out for the 'Blow Hole' here. At the right state of the tide water will rush through a hole eroded by the sea through the cliff and emerge as a fountain, making an awesome noise.

The path wanders round the cliff, uphill, but there are some welcome seats placed very strategically. Take a look at the sturdy little look-out tower on the headland of Willapark. The view from here is superb; to the north is Bude Bay, Hartland Point, and Lundy Island while to the south can be seen Tintagel and Trevose Head. The cliffs are sheer and there are warning notices of undercutting but this is certainly some of the finest cliff walking in Cornwall

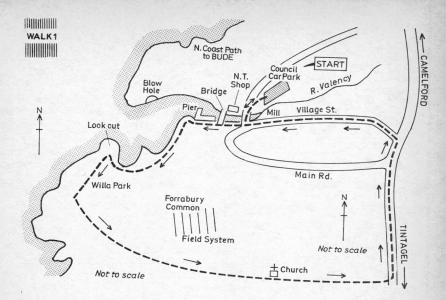

and it is said that Sir Henry Irving received the inspiration here to conceive the setting for one of his London productions.

Take the left hand path leading inland from the headland, across Forrabury Common with its evidence of an ancient field system, each plot or 'stitch' being a very long, narrow field of early medieval date. Take a look at Forrabury Church, where can be seen some Norman remains, an old cross in the churchyard and the weather vane on the tower in the form of a fish.

Forrabury Church has no bells. Legend has it that a set of bells were being brought by sea to be placed in the tower of the church and, after a pilot boarded the ship to navigate the narrow entrance to Boscastle harbour, a terrific storm sprang up. The ship bounced about on the massive waves but was mercifully intact when the storm abated. The pilot sank to his knees to thank God for their deliverance but the captain said, "You should be thanking me, not God, for bringing us to safety". Whereupon a huge wave engulfed the ship and it sank with all hands. Be the legend true or false, the fact remains that Forrabury Church is still without a ring of bells. There are some who say, however, that at certain tides the sound of bells can be heard mournfully peeling just off the rocks near to the church...

Leave the churchyard by the main gate and emerge on to the road from Tintagel. Turn left.

Cross over the next road to the left, leading to the harbour, and take the next turn left, signposted 'Village only'. This is a steep street lined with picturesque old cottages. After passing the

Methodist chapel and the primary school, the row of houses you come to on the right are built on the site of the old Bottreaux Castle, the castle of Boscastle.

The field just beyond the last of the houses suddenly takes on a semi-circular formation and dips sharply into the valley. Here is the site of the original earthen mound or motte on which the castle was built. Continue on through the village to the Wellington Inn and so over the bridge back to the car park.

Walk 2   **Nectan's Glen (between Tintagel and Boscastle)**

3 or 4 miles (4.75 or 6.5 km)

OS sheet 200

This walk cannot, strictly speaking, be called a coastal walk but I feel that I may be excused for including it in this book as it has been established that as early as 1799 travellers regarded the then-called 'Nathan's Cave' as one of the natural wonders of Cornwall. This later became known as Nectan's Kieve, kieve being the Cornish word for cauldron, bowl or basin and a name aptly used for the fall of water into a 'kieve'. The height of the fall is about 50 feet, dropping first into a granite basin, then through a rock cavity for its final fall into another stone basin and into the river. It is quite spectacular in its situation among overhanging trees and bushes.

Many are the stories associated with this romantic place; poets enthused over it, artists have painted it and some books tell us of an oratory or hermitage there. A house certainly stood at the entrance to the waterfall where, until recently, an ex-Guards NCO lived. Visitors to the glen could buy refreshments from him and be entertained by his talk on the wonders of this lovely place. His little house is now derelict, too 'far from it all' for most people to want to make a home there.

The valley is properly called Millcombe, but the top half is now called Nectan's Glen and the lower Rocky Valley.

The nearest town is Camelford and the route taken is by the well-signposted B3263 for Tintagel. On reaching Tintagel follow the sign for Bossiney and Boscastle, following the coast. Just through the hamlet of Bossiney the road goes steeply downhill round a sharp bend, then uphill. At the top of the hill is a hotel and almost opposite (on the left hand side of the road) is a car park. Leave the car here, cross the road and begin the walk to the left of the hotel.

The track is wide here. Notice after a few yards the ancient holy well on the left. A chapel of ease which lies ahead has been re-dedicated after being used as a cow-shed for many years. Turn right past the chapel, passing behind a nursery garden. The drive, wide now and surfaced in tarmac, leads to a few houses which are passed before entering the woods and valley. Keep to the right all the way. On entering the woods the path becomes slippery but is well defined.

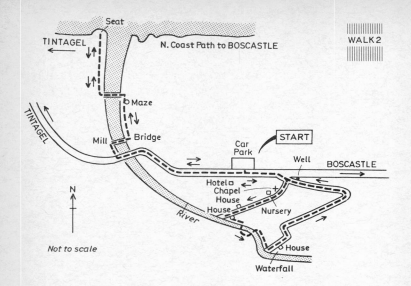

It leads gradually uphill, crossing the stream by a bridge at one place. It can be muddy here and is rather steep in places.

At the top of the hill are the remains of a house. Continue on, bearing to the right and eventually reaching a fence and gate on the right. There is a patio here, and this is where the café was situated. Walk down the rough steps, bearing to the left. A good view of the waterfall may be obtained from a ledge on the left of the stream or from a large flat rock midstream, reached by stepping stones. Whichever is chosen it will be very slippery.

To return, it is possible to use the lane which services the one or two cottages above the glen. Although this lane is rather longer than the woodland path the less sure-footed will probably prefer it to the downward journey through the woods. On reaching the car park keep going downhill, round the bend at the bottom, until a sign marked 'Footpath to Rocky Valley' is seen on the right. Take this path, past the old Trevillet Mill, now the house belonging to the trout farm where refreshments are offered throughout the summer. Cross the bridge and walk down the valley.

This was the last place in Cornwall where the Cornish Chough nested. This bird, with its characteristic red bill, is a member of the crow family and is now only to be found in captivity in the bird gardens of Cornwall. Rare and unusual flowers also abound here and 120 years ago the Killarney Fern was discovered.

The walk down this valley beside the rushing water is easy and pleasant. The old buildings are the remains of mills. About half-way down, just before crossing a bridge, take a look around at a derelict building which was a woollen mill. A woollen mill stood here whose

14

walls were built against the rock face. As the buildings gradually crumbled through the years of disuse most unusual carvings became exposed. Unique to Cornwall, they are cut into the slate behind the fallen granite wall of the mill. They are middle Bronze Age 'Maze' carvings, some 3,000 years old. Other engravings may be awaiting discovery among the confusion of rocks in this valley. Nobody can possibly know the origin of these markings but they are of Middle Eastern design and could have been the work of shipwrecked sailors who whiled away the winter months in this valley repairing their boat ready to put to sea again in the Spring.

Continue to walk down the valley until you reach the sea. At high tide the roar is deafening as the water enters the gorge. Climb the path up the cliff on the left for a wonderful coastline view. The return walk to the car is up the valley, turning left on reaching the road.

Walk 3   Tintagel Castle, Island and Church

3 miles (5 km)

OS sheet 200

Tintagel, known the world over for its association with the legendary King Arthur and the Knights of the Round Table, is a place to be visited during the comparatively peaceful months of Spring or Autumn. It is a mecca indeed for tourists and its popularity can cause some minor inconveniences during July and August.

The village itself is small and it straggles along one main street where cafés and gift shops hold pride of place. However, a good example of Tudor building may be seen in the Old Post Office, now owned by the National Trust. This was a manor house of the period and has an attractive well-preserved interior and a peaceful garden.

The castle building was begun by Reginald, Earl of Cornwall in the twelfth century and completed by the strange King Richard II. It has served as many things in its time, including a prison but it is not surprising that it has succumbed to the effects of several centuries of erosion in this exposed place.

Beyond the castle, on an isthmus known as the 'Island', is what, from an historical point of view, is the most interesting part of Tintagel — the monastery site dedicated to St Juliot. Founded about AD500 it was later extended by Celtic monks along the eastern side of the island. The castle and the monastery site are now in the care of the Department of the Environment and much work has been done to preserve these important ruins. The headland site was fitted for a stronghold and with its narrow neck to the mainland, its own water supply (the well is still there today), grazing for animals and escape routes by sea it certainly earned John Leland's title of unbeatable.

From the headland are some of the most dramatic cliff views of the north coast. The buzzard and the kestrel may be seen here, along with a variety of other sea birds, while the rock samphire and thrift are two attractive plants common to this part of the coast.

Barras Head, a promontory facing the castle, was the first piece of Cornwall to be given to the National Trust. Much of the Cornish coastline is now in their care, but in 1894, when speculative building was just beginning, it was thought that this beautiful headland was to be the next site for an hotel. Much concerned at this, a group of local artists raised the then princely sum of £505 by public subscription, purchased the land and gave it to the National Trust.

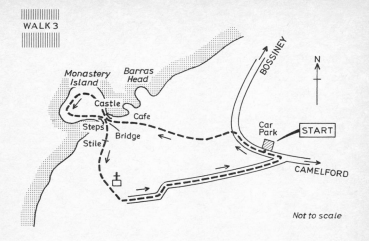

The directions for this walk are given from Camelford, the nearest town. Leave the town by the B3263 road signposted for Tintagel. The road twists and turns but is well signed all the way, about ten miles. On reaching the village there should be no difficulty in finding a car park. A good one to use is almost opposite the Old Post Office in the main street.

To start the walk, assuming that this park is used, turn right into the main street. In a few yards on the left is a sign marked 'To the Castle'. Take this rough track, going steeply downhill towards the beach. Keep to the main track all the way, ignore any paths off to the left. On reaching the path just above the beach, pause to look down and if the tide is low, walk into the cavern known as 'Merlin's Cave', running under the island. As the castle is in the care of the Department of the Environment an entrance fee must be paid before proceeding any further.

The approach to this Norman castle is over the bridge and up some steep steps into the outer ward. Pass through the gateway into the ruins and walk through the castle area into the monastery site. Notice the well, the chapel and the walled garden.

After leaving the island and re-crossing the bridge take the path leading to a flight of very steep steps. Climb these to the inner ward of the castle and then keep to the right where very shortly a sign marked 'To the Church' will be seen. Take this path which follows the coast, up a steep path, over a stile and out on to the open cliffs. Take any of the paths towards the church which lies just ahead. This Church of St Materiana was built almost exactly as it appears today with a cruciform shape of nave, chancel and transepts. It was built between the years of 1080 and 1150 in the time of the

17

first Norman Earls of Cornwall. While much of the fabric has been replaced, the font and three of the windows are Norman. The stone coffin of unusual length with a beautifully carved cross on the lid is probably of the time of Edward I.

After leaving the church through the main door, turn left on to a metalled road away from the coast. Walk along this road which bears left after a short distance and runs downhill steeply, passing the vicarage on the right. The road then goes uphill and joins the main street not far from the car park.

While this walk is not long, the interest it has to offer may tempt the walker to spend more time on it than a three mile walk usually takes.

Walk 4   Daymer Bay and Rock

3 miles (4.75 km)

OS sheet 200

Daymer Bay, an expanse of sand just in the Camel estuary, is a
paradise for children with its sand dunes, firm beach and sheltered
situation. However, it is in an estuary and care should be taken if
bathing. The famous, or rather infamous, Doom Bar, which
stretches across the mouth of this estuary has been the cause of many
shipwrecks. It is a stretch of sand which has formed over the years
and now effectively blocks the entrance to Padstow harbour for large
ships. The area is an important one for birdwatching and the dunes
support a wide variety of wild flowers.

The little Norman church of St Enodoc, which is one of the points
of interest along this walk, was buried in the sand for many years. It
was called locally 'Sinkininny' and when a service was held once a
year, access had to be made through a skylight by the vicar and
churchwarden. The church was restored in the nineteenth century
and services are now held there regularly. It is unusual in having a
steeple which is slightly crooked.

Rock is well-known as a sailing centre. It lies almost opposite
Padstow from which there is a ferry service. Padstow is the scene, on
May Day every year, of the Obby Oss festival, an ancient pagan
ceremony associated with fertility rites. It attracts large crowds
nowadays although originally it was just a village celebration.

The directions for the walk are given from Wadebridge, the
nearest town. Take the A39 Bude road until reaching the first set
of traffic lights then turn left on to the B3314. Continue on this
road for about five miles until a sign on the left marked 'Rock and
Pityme' is reached. Take this road but do not go into Rock village.
Just past an inn called Pityme is a turn to the right for Polzeath.
Take this road and after about a mile look for a sign on the left for
Daymer Bay. Turn into this lane, which is narrow, and leads down to
the beach and car park.

Part of this walk is over a golf course so care should be taken and
a watch kept for balls.

Leave the car on the park and walk back up the road a few yards
and look carefully for a sign in the hedge on the righthand side
marked St Enodoc Church. The path is wide and passes between
some lovely houses and gardens. In a little while it narrows and

19

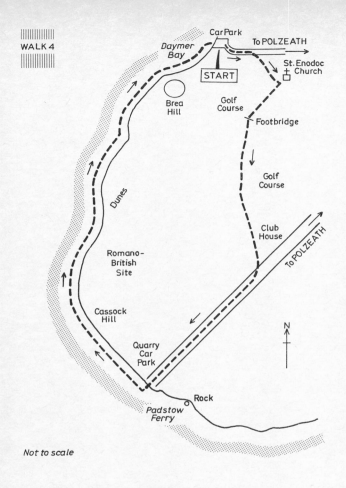

WALK 4

Car Park

To POLZEATH

Daymer Bay

St. Enodoc Church

START

Brea Hill

Golf Course

Footbridge

Dunes

Golf Course

Club House

To POLZEATH

Romano-British Site

Cassock Hill

N

Quarry Car Park

Rock

Padstow Ferry

Not to scale

crosses a bridge. The way to the church is now marked by white painted stones so the path is easy to follow. After leaving the church ascend a shallow valley alongside a stream, still following the white stones. Cross a small footbridge by a pond and bear left up the track. On reaching a tarmac road cross it diagonally and go through the bushes on to a path, marked by white posts, across the golf course. This joins the club house drive, at the end of which, turn right down the hill to Rock.

The walk back to Daymer Bay depends on the tide. If the tide is low it is possible to walk along the beach all the way but if it is high or rising it is as well to follow the marked path through the sand dunes parallel with the shore.

20

Walk 5   Newquay and Watergate Bay

5½ miles (9 km)

OS sheet 200

If you propose to walk on the beach, in either direction, consult the tide table and allow yourself three hours before high water.

The walk begins at the major holiday resort of Newquay, a busy town which developed from a very small fishing village known as Towan Blystra. The inhabitants of the village spent their time catching shoals of pilchards which invaded the area of Newquay Bay during the autumn months. The fish were then salted and prepared for export to Latin countries to be eaten during Lent. For some reason, during the late nineteenth century, the pilchards failed to follow their usual routes and the fishing industry fell into decline. Mackerel and shell fish are still caught in Newquay Bay, however, and fishermen augment their income by taking holidaymakers on sightseeing and fishing trips during the summer months.

It was fortunate that the decline in the fishing industry coincided with the arrival of the railway in Cornwall as this enabled the county to welcome more visitors and brought a new way of life to the local people.

Newquay has seven of the most beautiful beaches in the county. The Atlantic Ocean laps its shores making it a surfer's paradise and the golden sands a child's dream.

It is very necessary to watch the tide carefully for this walk if using the beach it either direction. Allow at least three hours before high water for the beach walk.

Newquay has many car parks but, for this walk, the one adjacent to the railway station is the most convenient. Approaching the town from the north on the A392 road, follow the signs marked 'Town Centre'. Travel along Narrowcliff, past all the big hotels until a sign on the left marked 'Railway Station' is reached. Just past this is a turn to the left; take this and the car park is almost immediately on the left.

After leaving the car, walk back into the main street and turn right towards the Great Western Hotel. Continue walking along the footpath above the beach parallel with the hotels. The outward walk is given along the cliffs but the direction can be reversed if the tide is more suitable for the beach walk. On reaching a shelter at the end of the promenade turn left towards the sea. Do not go down on to the beach but bear right across the open cliffs, in an area known as the Barrowfields. This name is self-explanatory for the

21

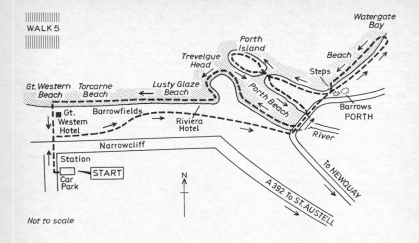

Not to scale

barrows are very much in evidence.

On reaching the Riviera Hotel, bear left and then turn left at the road junction. Follow the path downhill on to Porth Beach but keep to the back of the beach as the river crossing is only possible by the road. After crossing the river continue on the pavement uphill until a signpost marked 'Coastal Footpath' is reached. Take this path and follow it all the way to Watergate Bay, passing two large barrows *en route*. There are adequate facilities for refreshment on reaching the beach area.

The walk back is along the beach until a promontory known as Porth Island is reached. It is very difficult to negotiate the rocks here and the best route is up a steep flight of steps at Whipsiderry Beach. The steps terminate on the road above the beach. Walk down the road until reaching the pitch and putt course entrance gate. It is now possible to make a diversion on to Porth Island, or Trevelgue head to give it its proper name. This Iron Age promontory fort offers many interesting features. The bank and ditch fortification is thought to be one of the best preserved in the country. There is a large Bronze Age barrow dominating the headland and a spectacular blow-hole in the left-hand angle of the rocks.

Returning to Porth Beach again, and carefully watching the tide, walk seawards and round the rocks to reach Lusty Glaze beach. The way should be clear now and the walking easy across the wide open sandy beaches. Tolcarne is the next beach and it has several rows of bathing huts. Following this is Great Western Beach and from here the ascent to the town is made. Walk up the slope to the left of the beach and emerge on to a footpath a few yards from the Great Western Hotel. Turn right and in a few yards the car park can be seen almost opposite.

Walk 6   Newquay and East Pentire

3½ miles (5.25 km)

OS sheet 200

A second walk in the Newquay area is a must as this busy resort
has much to commend it. The vehicle can be left in the car park
adjacent to the railway station, as described in the previous walk,
but the route taken is in the opposite direction.

On leaving the car park walk into the main street where,
immediately opposite, is a track between two hotels. Take this track,
which was the old tramway track leading to the harbour. It was
along this route that the minerals were carried after being trans-
ported by tramway from the south coast. The tramway was
constructed in the early nineteenth century by the then local squire,
named Trefrye, who also built the extra quay in the centre of the
harbour to facilitate the loading and unloading of the trucks. This
quay was joined to the mainland by a wooden structure supporting
the tramway. The Great Western Railway used parts of the old
tramway when bringing the railway into Cornwall. The track now
being used for the walk is all that remains of it in Newquay.

Newquay was originally called Towan Blystra and it was in the
sixteenth century that Bishop Lacey gave the money for the
construction of a new quay to provide a harbour; from this the name
Newquay evolved.

On reaching the end of the track, turn right, past the bus
station, on to an open grassed area known as the Killacourt.
There are several paths across and they all lead down to Towan
Beach. If the tide is low, descend to the beach and turn left
towards the harbour wall. If the tide is high then follow the footpaths
skirting the beach and take the signs for the harbour. On reaching
the harbour take a look at the inshore lifeboat, much used during the
summer months to rescue foolhardy holidaymakers. The adjacent
rowing club houses the gigs, long rowing boats now only used for
competition racing although in the early part of the century they
were still being used as pilot boats to guide ships safely into harbour.

If the tide is low, walk across the beach; if not, it is necessary to
climb the hill, turn right at the top into Fore St and then first right
by the Red Lion inn and so join the path leading from the harbour
beach. Continue seawards along the tarmac road, at the end of
which is a flight of steps. Ascend these and on reaching the open

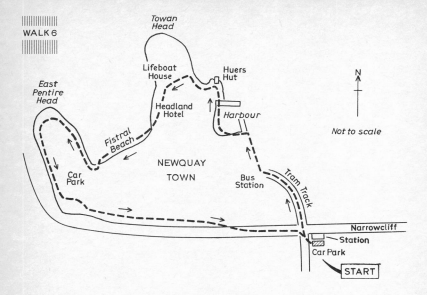

cliff take any of the paths across the clifftop, aiming at a white building ahead.

This is the Huer's Hut, so called from the pilchard-fishing days. A 'huer' would scan the bay for the shoals of pilchard approaching the shores during the months of August-October. On sighting the fish he would alert the village with a cry of 'Heva, Heva' and the boats would then take to sea and encircle the shoal with a seine net. When the fish were brought to the beach, the rest of the inhabitants would help to land them and then cure the catch for storing for their own use during the winter or for export.

After leaving the hut, follow the tarmac road to the right. In about 300 yards the road bends to the left and a footpath leads off to the right. Take the path which leads out on to the headland. On reaching the old lifeboat house, now disused, turn left in front of the Headland Hotel. Ahead lies the vast expanse of Fistral Beach, another famous beach where international surfing competitions are held. It is usually possible to walk across the sands at any state of the tide but there is a footpath through the dunes if preferred.

After crossing the beach, ascend a flight of steps on to a road. Turn right here and use the road, which gradually deteriorates into a track, passing some bungalows on the left. Continue walking uphill until an open space and car park are reached. This headland is known as East Pentire and the views across Crantock Beach to the left and the river Gannel estuary are superb.

The walk back into town is necessarily through the built-up area of East Pentire but this has compensations as the footpath is wide and the district very pleasant. The road from the headland goes inland for about a mile. On reaching a junction of four roads, take the left hand, uphill, one. At the top, turn left into Atlantic Road. This road bends right at the bottom and almost immediately comes to a cross roads. Cross straight over into Crantock Street which leads back into the town centre where it is easy to retrace the route back to the car park.

Walk 7   Crantock and Porth Joke

4 miles (6.5 km)

OS sheet 200

Crantock is situated off the A3075 Newquay to Redruth road.
Directions are given from Newquay.

Leave the town by the A3075 towards Redruth. Take the first
right turn after crossing Trevemper Bridge over the river Gannel.
Turn right at the next cross roads and then first right into Crantock
village. Keep left on reaching the village square, taking the road
signposted 'To the Beach'. There is a National Trust car park
adjacent to the beach and a private one a few yards up the road.

The view from the NT car park is blocked by sand dunes and
the movement of the sand throughout the winter is causing much
concern to the local authorities. A programme of marram grass
planting has been taking place in an effort to stabilize the area.

Leave the car park by the path behind the toilets. Keep to the left
at the top of the hill as there is a maze of paths leading through the
dunes towards the beach which do not make for comfortable
walking. The dunes give way to farmland after about half a mile and
the path goes round the edge of two cultivated fields. The view from
here is magnificent. Given the right conditions, the sea could be alive
with the black dots of the members of a surfing club. Look down
from the cliffs to the beach below where huge sea caverns have been
formed by the continuous aerial and sea erosion. The colours in the
slates are quite beautiful. These rocks were formed during the
Devonian period approximately 350 million years ago. The quartz
veins running through them were produced at the time of the granite
intrusion.

The path now descends by steps to a footbridge, then uphill,
bearing to the left. At a junction of paths keep to the right, passing
in front of the lawns of the Crantock Bay Hotel. Keeping always to
the path nearest to the sea continue on to the headland known as
West Pentire Point. There is nice springy turf to walk on here and
the path is easy to follow right down into Porth Joke. This porth,
or beach, is National Trust owned, as are the surrounding cliffs.
Even at the height of the season one can enjoy reasonable seclusion
here, no doubt due to the absence of any amenities.

Cross over the footbridge and take the path leading to the left and
inland. This leads to Cubert Common where Bronze Age barrows

26

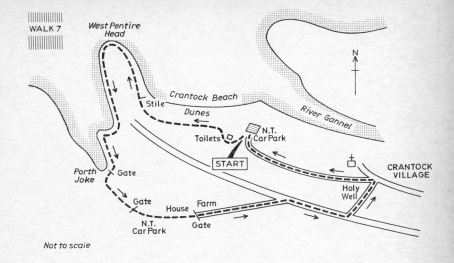

Not to scale

may be seen. Legend has it that if any of these are disturbed disaster will befall the village of Cubert. Strangely enough they are all still intact so perhaps legend has its uses after all.

On reaching a gate and the National Trust car park turn left on to a wide track. After about a quarter of a mile the track ends with a gate leading on to a tarmac road. Turn left here and continue uphill until reaching a T junction. Turn right and after a short distance bear left. This road leads back into Crantock village.

The village itself deserves more than a glance. The church is noted for its exceptional carvings, both of the screen and the bench-ends. Take a look at the stocks at the side of the church and the unusual stone coffin in the churchyard. There is a holy well in the centre of the village and another one, dedicated to St Ambrose, half way down the road to the beach. A visit to the Albion Inn, apart from being sustaining, can prove interesting for this old hostelry could tell many a tale of bygone smugglers. A warm welcome is afforded to present day travellers both by 'mine host' and an open fire.

The walk ends with a gentle stroll back to the car.

Walk 8   Perranporth to Trevellas Coombe

6½ miles (10.5 km)

OS sheet 204

Perranporth, famed for its two miles of sandy beaches, is an active holiday resort. Its vast expanse of sand is used for the sport of land yachting and the Atlantic waves for surfing. The beach is backed by a range of sand dunes which stretch for miles. Among them is the lost church of St Piran. This oratory, which had been buried under the sand, was uncovered due to the shifting of the sand during the nineteenth century. It is believed to be the oldest church building, being of the sixth century. With its exposure to the elements it began to deteriorate very quickly, a deterioration helped by human hands seeking souvenirs. The little church was eventually protected by a concrete shell which afforded sufficient cover until 1981 when there was further encroachment by both sand and water. After much discussion the parish council decided to re-bury it with sand and only a cross now marks the spot where this lonely church lies hidden.

Directions for this walk are given from Newquay. Leave the town by the Redruth road, the A3075. On reaching the village of Goon-havern after about eight miles, turn right, signposted 'Perranporth'. Follow this road into the town and on reaching a cross roads turn right towards the sea. The car park adjacent to the beach is the most convenient one to use.

After leaving the car, take the road leading uphill over the cliff to another car park at the top; walk diagonally across this towards Droskyn Hall. Turn right behind the hotel where there is a wide track. Pass a coastguard look-out in a little while and the track then narrows to a path. There is much evidence of quarrying here and some large caves. The path is rather rough in places and near the edge so care should be taken, particularly after heavy rain. Called the 'North Coast Footpath', it continues down some steps, over a stile and eventually comes out on to Cligga Head.

This is an area famed for its geology, a site much used by mineralogists, collectors and geologists from all over the world. Such minerals as cassiterite (tin), wolfram and some good quartz specimens can be collected. However, it is rather a desolate part of the coast with the remains of buildings used during the last war littering the waste ground. A glider and light aircraft base is situated

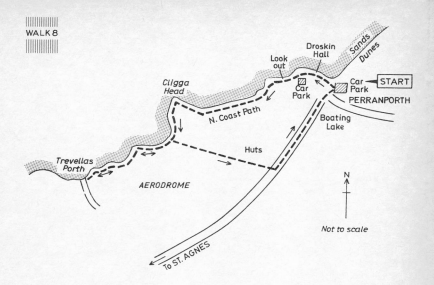

here and concrete paths lead across the open spaces. Care should be taken to keep to the coastal path and follow the cliff edge closely.

Leaving Cligga Head behind, the path is easily defined down into Trevellas Coombe, a pretty spot with a pebbly beach which is dangerous for bathing. There are some quite well preserved mine engine houses in the vicinity and it is easy to see that much mining took place here at one time.

The walk back necessitates retracing the path to Cligga Head from which point it is possible to vary the route back into Perranporth. Either follow the coast path all the way (the scenery is so different when walking in the opposite direction) or take one of the concrete roadways across the open waste land towards the road. On joining the road, turn left and walk downhill into Perranporth, passing the boating lake and other recreational sites on the way.

Walk 9   Chapel Porth - St Agnes - Chapel Porth

3 miles (5 km)

OS sheet 203

Cornwall's north coast at its most spectacular. This cliff area is steep and rugged, littered with mining remains. The village of St Agnes is worthy of a visit, particularly the church and the Railway Inn. During re-flooring work to the former in 1931 traces of early structures, 12ft by 18ft, were revealed, probably a pre-Norman chapel. The latter is famed for its collection of shoes; they are of all kinds and there are dozens of them, from dancing shoes to clogs.

The beach for St Agnes is known as Trevaunance Cove and is about a mile from the village. St Agnes Beacon, which dominates this area, is a high granitic outcrop; hence the mineralisation of the surrounding district. There are Bronze Age barrows on the summit and it is here that one in the chain of bonfires is lit on special occasions and on Midsummer Eve. It is said to be possible to see 30 church towers or spires on a clear day from this point.

The nearest town is Redruth. Take the A30 Redruth-Bodmin Road through the village of Blackwater, up a hill to a roundabout. Turn left here on to the B3277 for St Agnes. The approach to the village passes the St Agnes Model Village and just past here is a turn to the left, signposted 'Chapel Porth'. Take this road, which skirts St Agnes Beacon, following the signs for Chapel Porth. The approach road to the beach is steep and narrow but there are passing places. Park the car in the National Trust car park almost on the beach and you will notice that above the car park, on the cliffside, the words 'Chapel Porth' have been worked in white stones.

The walk starts by leaving the car park and with the sea on the left take the steep path from the road up on to the cliffs. The path is easily defined and is close to the cliff edge. It goes downhill after a while, crossing a small stream. From here keep left — do not take the wide track leading off to the right. Climb up the next cliff, which is rather steep, but the view from the top makes it very worthwhile. Follow the coast closely and continue walking until the first engine house is reached. This is the engine house for the Towan Roath shaft of Wheal Coates mine and has been restored by the National Trust. It also forms the frontispiece for Daphne du Maurier's book *Vanishing Cornwall.*

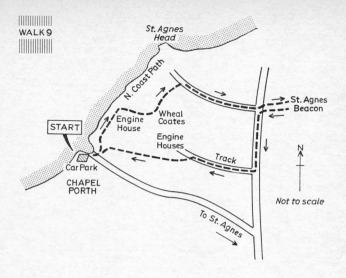

There are many tracks leading from here to the top of the cliff where the remains of Wheal Coates mine buildings may be seen. Take any of these tracks rather than continuing on the coastal footpath. On reaching the top, turn left and follow the wide track over the headland. After about a quarter of a mile take a path leading diagonally across the open cliff to the right. This leads to a tarmac road used only for access to the headland and the coastguard look-out post. Turn right here and follow the road until a T junction is reached. Cross the road and take the path almost opposite leading to the top of St Agnes Beacon.

The views from here are splendid, with the rugged coastline on the one side and the 'Cornish Alps', as the china clay tips are called, in the distance to the south. Carn Brea, another granitic outcrop, surmounted by its castle and monument, dominates the skyline in the near distance.

Use the same path to descend from the beacon and when the road is rejoined, turn left and walk on for about half a mile until a track leading off to the right is reached. This is rough but wide enough for a car and leads down to Wheal Coates. Just before reaching the mine buildings, bear left and follow the track all the way back into Chapel Porth.

Walk 10

Portreath - Porthtowan - Portreath

7 miles (11 km)

OS sheet 203

This walk is steeper and longer than most and should, therefore, only be attempted by the more experienced walker.

Portreath is a small holiday village now, but in times past was an important harbour for this dangerous North Coast. It was known as Bassett's Cove, after the family of prominent mineral lords of the district who established the harbour to export tin and copper ore and import coal. Minerals were carried by pack mules until 1810 when the horse-drawn tramway was established. This was closed down about 1870 by which time copper exports had ceased. Part of our walk is along the old mineral railway track. Before leaving the village take a look at the harbour and notice the day-mark known locally as the 'Pepper-pot', on the cliff.

A day-mark is a tower, and day-marks vary much in shape according to their location. Some of them are very high, for example the one at Gribben Head where it commands an important site marking the entrance to St Austell Bay and to Fowey. Another, at Stepper Point where it marks the entrance to Padstow harbour, looks almost like an engine house chimney. The 'Pepper Pot' is much smaller, is painted white and is indeed shaped just like a pepper pot. It marks the entrance to Portreath harbour and acts as a guide to shipping in the area. The name 'day-mark' is used as these towers do not have lights and so cannot be confused with a lighthouse with its all-important navigational beam.

Redruth is the nearest town and directions are taken from there. Take the B3330 road out of the town, well signposted for Portreath. The road goes down into the village along the valley and a car park and refreshment and toilet facilities will be found close to the beach. For those interested in collecting stones some good examples of banded agates are to be found on the beach here.

To begin the walk, take the road used to enter the village back towards Redruth. From the village square in front of the Portreath Hotel walk on to the end of the village. Opposite the school turn left and then take the footpath almost immediately on the right. This is the old tramway track which once went to Scorrier with its trucks full of coal and returned loaded with ore. The path is easy to follow

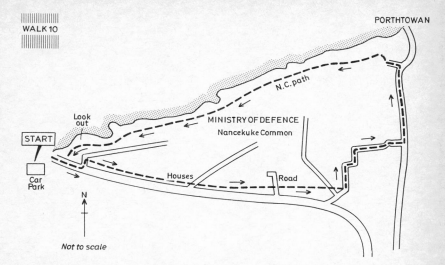

and supports a wealth of wild flowers along the hedgerows. At one point, where there is a fork, there are some houses. The tramway is the lower, or right hand, path. It crosses over a road and a lane before emerging on to a tarmac road. Carry straight on, taking the higher road and at the junction turn left.

Follow this lane up the hill but look back while pausing for breath and admire the view across to Carn Brea. At the top of the hill the road bends sharp right and begins to descend, turning left then right. Halfway up the next slope turn left and follow this road, passing an old school house on the way. At the T junction turn right and at the next T junction turn left. Continue walking along this road until Porthvean Crescent is reached. Just past this crescent a rough track leads on to the cliffs above Porthtowan.

A detour into Porthtowan can be made here. Instead of taking the track to the cliffs continue down the hill, turning left at the bottom into the village and to the beach. The coastal path can be joined by taking the cliff road leading left from the beach. Whichever route is chosen the North Coast path is easy to follow all the way back to Portreath.

There are two very steep dips shortly after leaving Porthtowan. The scenery is superb, the sea birds in the proper environment are beautiful and the Atlantic breakers on a windy day quite breath-taking. Wild flowers abound and for those interested in Cornwall's mining past much evidence of its activity can be seen. The Ministry of Defence have a site here, hence the wire fence which the coastal footpath skirts.

The path emerges opposite the Gull Rock Hotel and it is not far downhill to the car park.

Walk 11   Carbis Bay to St Ives

4 miles (6.5 km)

OS sheet 203

This walk offers firm and sheltered paths and is, therefore, very suitable for windy or damp days.

Directions are given from Hayle on the A30 Redruth-Penzance road. Leave Hayle, a name which is Cornish for estuary, on the A30 Penzance road. After about one mile notice the area of water on the right, the estuary of the river Hayle and a well-known bird-watching spot. You will almost certainly see heron, black backed gulls, oyster catchers and other waders. Take the right turn almost immediately past here, signed 'Lelant and St Ives'. Notice the old Custom House, now an hotel, on the right at a point which boats would have been able to reach before the silting of the river occurred.

Turn right again after passing Lelant Model Village and continue on this road to Carbis Bay. After passing a motel on the right look out for Porthrepta Road on the right hand side. Take this turn and, immediately after passing the church, turn left into a car park, the nearest park to the beach.

Make your way down the hill to Carbis Bay beach. Keeping to the path above the beach and through a private car park, pass over a bridge and up a flight of steps. The view of the bay from here is quite spectacular with Gwithian sands and the Godrevy lighthouse in the distance.

Continue uphill until reaching a metalled road, turn right, passing between several very nice houses, and on coming to a sign 'Pedestrians only' on the right, take this path, downhill, until a five-barred gate is reached on the right. This has a National Trust plaque marking Porthminster Point. Pass over a very low granite stile beside the gate, then under a railway bridge. The path here leads to the right but after a few yards take a left fork on to the coastal footpath. Keep to the top path nearest to the railway line. On reaching another bridge turn left and cross a bridge over the railway. Then turn right, past a house called Chy and Carrack. Turn right immediately after the house and take the lower concrete path. Turn right at the next junction towards Porthminster beach, passing over a metal bridge on the way.

Take the path through the gardens, where refreshments may be

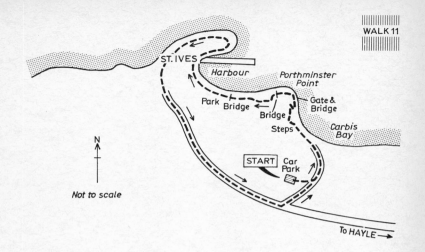

obtained. At the end of the gardens, do not ascend the steps but keep straight on into an area known as The Warren, past the Lamplighter Studio and into the harbour area. This is a pretty part of St Ives, with very narrow streets and colour-washed houses. Continue straight on into the town, following the coastline.

I would not presume to guide you through the town. It is sufficient to say that wherever one looks there is something unusual and very individual. The museum is a place of immense interest and it must be a pleasure to walk out on to Smeaton's Pier. The inn called The Sloop, on the harbour side, has quite a history and a walk out on to the island with its little fishermen's chapel can be rewarding. It is small wonder that St Ives is an artists' paradise.

The walk back to the car has to follow the same route unless road walking is preferred. In this case just follow the road signs back to Carbis Bay.

In retracing the coast path, small variations can be made by crossing the beach at Porthminster should the tide be low. Another deviation can be made a little further on and this does make a short cut. Do not cross the railway bridge at the top of the hill above the beach but keep straight on until the original drive is joined once again.

Walk 12   Levant and Botallack

3 miles (4.75 km)

OS sheet 203

Directions for this walk are given from Penzance. Take the A3071 road to St Just. On reaching the village, pass by the village square and church on the right and continue straight on, taking the B3306 road for Morvah and St Ives. At the village of Trewellard, take the left turn in the centre of the village, which leads down to Levant Mine. The lane ends on the cliffs where there is ample car parking space.

Before commencing the walk take a look at the old engine house of Levant Mine. This was the scene of a tragic accident on 20 October 1919 when a cap on the engine above ground snapped and 31 men, who were being brought up the shaft, hurtled to their death below ground. The inquest verdict was 'Accidental death caused by the breakage of a strap-plate due to metal fatigue'. A few lucky survivors have told of their miraculous escape. This was only one of many accidents which occurred during the time when very early machinery was used. The National Trust now cares for the engine house and permission can be obtained to go inside. (Apply to Geevor Tin Mine in advance.)

For the walk turn left, or away, from the engine house. Follow the coastal footpath which takes the form of a wide track at this point. It continues to be easily defined but always keep to the widest path nearest to the coast. The wild rocky coastline scenery here is very grand, and mining waste dumps, where many minerals can still be found, are also to be seen. After walking for about one mile and passing a derelict house on the left, the track becomes 'made up' and the approach is made to Botallack Head.

There is evidence here of modern mining where a new shaft has been opened in connection with Geevor Mine, the only working mine in this part of Cornwall. Look down the cliffs to see the spectacular siting of the Crowns engine houses. They have inspired many artists and photographers and it is easy to see why, particularly when the Atlantic rollers are dashing against the rocks. It is here that Prince Edward and Princess Alexandra went underground, indeed under the sea bed, to see the conditions experienced by the miners of their day. Today there remain only the shells of the engine houses, in

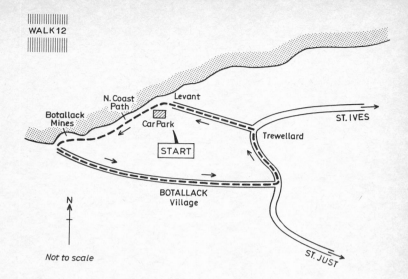

themselves a memorial to the men of that era. Take the path down the cliff for a closer look should you be feeling energetic.

Continue the walk by passing the Old Count House, now a restaurant, following the road to the left. The old house on the left, just past the Count House, was used in the filming of the Poldark series for television. This road leads into the village of Botallack where there is an inn but no other refreshment facilities.

It is now necessary either to retrace the coastal footpath or take the road back to Trewellard. The road is not busy, except in the height of the season, and it makes a pleasant walk with Madron Moor towering on the right and the view across the fields to the left. On reaching Trewellard village, take the left turn again and so back to the car.

Walk 13   St Just area

6 miles (9.5 km)

OS sheet 203

The area around St Just was once the scene of tin and copper mining and many vivid reminders of the past are to be seen in the tall engine houses which contained the engines to pump the water from the mines. The working tin mine of Geevor is situated a few miles along the road to Pendeen and visitors can see mining relics and present day methods of extracting the ore in the adjacent museum.

St Just lies seven miles from Penzance and directions are given from there. Take the A3071 road, signposted St Just, out of the town. On reaching the village leave the car in the central square or in the car park just to the left of it. Whilst in the village take the opportunity to look at the church where fifth century wall paintings of Christ of the Trades and of St George and the Dragon can be seen. A pillar stone with the Chi-Rho monogram is an unusual feature.

Just to the left of the village square is a grassed area of a Medieval Round, a site where miracle plays were performed and meetings took place; indeed, even today, it is the scene of folk festivals and the like.

From the car park take the signposted road marked Cape Cornwall and in a few minutes a sign to Carn Gloose will be seen. Follow this single track road and join the coastal path to Cape Cornwall. The only Cape in England, it has an engine house chimney on its summit. St Helen's Oratory was situated at the foot of the Cape and outlines of the buildings can still be seen in the field. After walking out on to the Cape, well worthwhile for the views, take the metalled road up the hill.

Where the road bears right, turn left below the wall of Porthleddon Hotel. Continue along the valley side for nearly a mile until the path reaches Boscean Farm. Here, turn left down to a stream, over the bridge, then left again along the track to the summit of Kenidjack Cliff.

Just before the quarry, turn right up a steep path to the summit. Continue along the high level path around the cliff top to Botallack Head. To continue the walk, after perhaps visiting the Crown Houses described in the previous walk, it is necessary to retrace the path back as far as the valley, known as the Tregaseal Valley. Turn left here

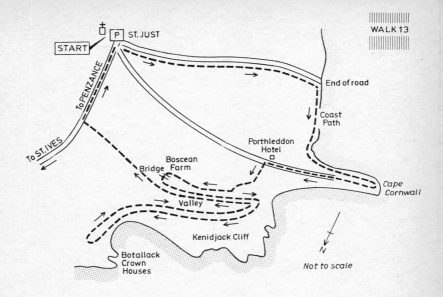

and follow the track all the way to the road.

On reaching the road, turn right, up a steep hill, and so back to the village and car park.

Walk 14   Sennen Cove and Land's End

4 miles (6.5 km)

OS sheet 203

Land's End, the most westerly point of England, must always be a magnet to draw the crowds, whether they be British or foreign. In Roman times both Diodoras and Ptolemy referred to Land's End as Bolerium, the seat of storms. Today, the seas still crash against the granite rocks and the Longships lighthouse is bathed in spray. There are, indeed, few days in the year when all is calm at Land's End. To the Cornish it was known as 'Pen Von Las', the End of the Earth. Wesley preached here, Turner visited it to sketch and paint and George Bernard Shaw came here to write.

Land's End, or Peal Point, is suffering from the ravages of time. The many pilgrims to this spot have left their mark and the conservationists are using their skills to find a solution to the problem. The estate of Charles Neave Hill, which includes Land's End, was sold in 1982 and its future is being watched with interest by many people.

Sennen Cove is guarded by the headland of Pedn-men-Dhu and, more southerly, by Mayon Cliff. The village is delightful. Within the sweep of Whitesand Bay it is a surfer's paradise — and the lifeboat which serves this treacherous area is housed here. An unusual round building above the beach was the capstan house which housed the machinery, turned by donkeys, used to pull the boats up the steeply shelved beach. It has recently had some much needed repair work attended to, for this is a place of historical interest.

Sennen village, on the A30, is situated above the cove. The church, dedicated in 1441, owes its origin to St Senan, a priest who reached Cornwall from Ireland in about the sixth century. Not far from the church is the Table-mên, a block of granite 7ft 10in long. Legend has it that at this stone seven Saxon kings dined after defeating the Danes at Villan Druacher about AD600. Merlin prophesied that peace will return to the earth when seven kings dine here again.

The directions for this walk are given from Penzance, the nearest town. Take the A30 Land's End road from the town, clearly signposted. Follow this all the way to the car park on the headland, a distance of about 10 miles.

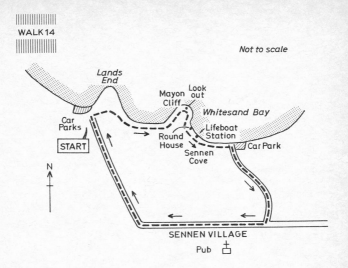

Leave the car and walk away from the hotel towards the First and Last House passing one or two souvenir shops on the way and the photographer with his signpost giving mileages from this spot to places all over the world. There are numerous paths along the coast and after passing the First and Last House take the most convenient one away from the headland to join up with the coastal footpath. This is well defined and easy to follow although there are some boggy places. The Isles of Scilly which lie 28 miles off Land's End can often be seen from here. Mayon Cliff ahead has a coastguard look-out post on the Pedn men dhu headland.

The path descends steeply into the village of Sennen Cove and enters it through a car park. The round house is situated here.

Walk across the car park and along the village street, passing the lifeboat house on the left. Here the full beauty of Whitesand Bay delights the eye with Cape Cornwall in the distance. Just to the south of the Cape lie the Brison Rocks, the scene of many a tragic shipwreck in days of sail. For the botanist, a detour along the beach to the lifeguard hut should prove worthwhile. Here may be seen, among other flora, the lovely sea holly.

The village street passes an hotel and then climbs very steeply uphill out of the village. This road is winding and there is not a pavement so care should be taken. On reaching the top, turn right into Sennen village. The church is on the left and the First and Last Inn just past it. Continue on through the village, following the main road all the way back to the car park at Land's End.

41

Walk 15

Lamorna — Tater-du lighthouse — Lamorna

5 miles (8 km)

OS sheet 203

This walk is rather steep in places and can be wet after heavy rain.

The directions for Lamorna are taken from Penzance. Take the coast road from Penzance to Newlyn and then the B3315 for Lamorna, turning left after about six miles (signposted). Leave the car in the car park at Lamorna Cove.

The walk passes through bulb fields, includes an old cross and a prehistoric stone circle, standing stones and a burial site.

Take the footpath to the right of the car park and follow the path for a few hundred yards—some clambering over boulders which have fallen and blocked the path is necessary here—but very soon the 'Silent Cross of Lamorna' comes into sight. Below a vast pile of lichen-covered rocks stands this granite cross. It is about five feet high and has no name, no inscription, no date. It is set on a levelled rock and stands there, a silent tribute to something or someone.

After passing the cross continue to follow the coastal path along Tregurrow Cliff up a steep stepped path on to Rosemodress Cliff. There is a stile at the top, then a steep downhill before ascending again to pass through the bulb fields. Here are grown early daffodils and narcissi which present a pretty picture in early Spring. The path is easy to follow and comes out on to a track leading to Tater-du lighthouse, an unmanned light which is operated in conjunction with Lizard light.

Up the track behind the lighthouse a gate is reached. The coastal footpath continues to the left on towards Land's End, but this walk takes the wide track past a house on the right which used to be a series of coastguard cottages. Continue along the lane to Boscowen Rose Farm. Passing the farm to the right the lane bears left and then right and continues on to join the B3315 at a T junction.

It is necessary from this point to use the roads back to Lamorna. Turn right at the T junction where, almost immediately on the right, is an ancient Megalithic chamber tomb. This came to light during road widenings and it is to the County Council's credit that a good job was made of protecting it. It is now in the care of the Department of the Environment.

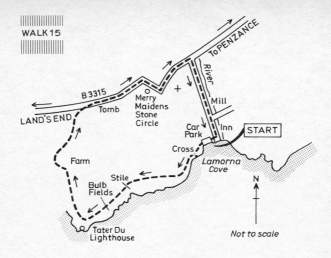

The next field on **the right past the tomb** is the location of the best known of the Cornish stone circles, known as the 'Merry Maidens', so called because they are said to be girls who were turned into stone for dancing on a Sunday. The two large standing stones at the top of the hill on the left are said to be the two pipers who were playing for them.

Continue along the road until the next right turn for Lamorna. This is the road used earlier during the car journey to the cove. Now is the time to notice the trees, flowers, shrubs and the beautiful cottages which flank the lane, making this one of the loveliest valleys in Cornwall. The old mill and the inn can be visited on the way back to the cove. Artists frequent this valley and small studios offer visitors the opportunity to purchase pictures as lasting mementos of this Cornish haven.

43

Walk 16   Mousehole to Lamorna

5½ miles (9 km)

OS sheet 203

Directions for this walk are given from Penzance. Take the coast road from Penzance signposted 'Newlyn and Mousehole'. Pass through Newlyn, noting the harbour-side fish warehouses and the newly built pier, opened by HM The Queen in 1981, to afford better harbour facilities for the Cornish fishing fleet. The road winds its way through narrow streets and past Penlee Quarry where road stone is extracted, much of it to be despatched by sea. The next village is Mousehole and the most convenient place to park is just before entering the village, on the left hand side where there is a large council car park.

Leave the car and take the exit from the park in the right hand corner. This leads on to a path almost on the shore. Turn right, towards the village, and follow the path into another car park. Cross this and into the main street.

Mousehole is a typical Cornish fishing village with narrow, winding streets and old houses in little alleyways. The colourwashed cottages are a delight and the Ship Inn a typical fishermen's hostelry. The village was the home of Dolly Pentreath, the lady reputed to be the last person to use the Cornish language as her native tongue, and the remains of her cottage can be seen. There are many artists' studios and other craft workshops.

When you have explored Mousehole to your satisfaction start the walk by taking the road past the chapel and up a steep hill past the bird sanctuary, a visit to which can prove rewarding. At the top of the hill the road levels out and after passing two very pretty cottages there is a sign on the left marked 'Footpath to Lamorna'.

This is the old coastguard's path and, in fact, still leads to a look-out post, manned only when a gale stronger than Force 4 is blowing. The path runs through flower fields where daffodils grow wild, bluebells carpet the cliffs and primroses nestle in the long grass while the tiny protected fields on the left of the path are used for cultivating the very early violets and anenomes.

The path is much walked and easy to follow. Great flat granite rocks flank the shore and make an ideal spot for fishing or sunbathing. After about one mile the path enters a wood, most

44

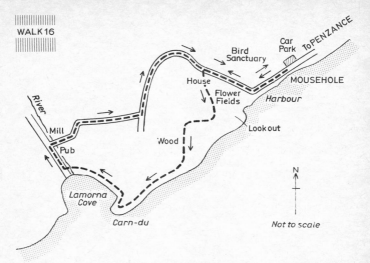

unusual on a coastal footpath. On emerging, climb the stile and continue along for a short distance and then round the headland. The path is near the edge in places here and some boulders have to be climbed over. On turning the corner, Lamorna comes into sight. Although it may look only a few minutes' walk away there is, in fact, still some quite hard walking to be done. The boulders are many and care should be taken.

The entrance into Lamorna is past a granite quarry, now disused, but stone from it was used to build the Thames Embankment in London. Lamorna Cove, a mere cluster of cottages fronting a stoney shore and deep blue sea, is, I think, every Cornishman's dream of home.

On reaching the car park, turn right up the rather steep road which leads to the village. The old inn, known as The Wink is on the right and immediately past it is a turn to the right. Just on a bridge, enter a garden wilderness where water plants of vast proportions may be seen. This is the Old Mill which has a working water wheel for generating electricity and a small craft shop. The river valley was at some time in the past treamed for tin. Traces of workings may still be found and quite a few semi-precious stones such as amethyst and agate can be found amongst the gravel. The valley has, more lately, been used for flower farming.

There is a footpath back to Mousehole along the roads and over the fields or you can just follow the road up the hill, turning left out of the Old Mill. It is well-signposted back to Mousehole. Personally, I think to retrace one's steps along the coast is much the best, as all the things missed on the outward trek can be appreciated on the way back.

45

Walk 17 St Michael's Mount and Penzance

6 miles (9.5 km)

OS sheet 203

A check with the tide chart must be made before crossing the causeway to St Michael's Mount as it is uncovered only at certain states of the tide. For information—particularly in the winter when the ferry may not operate—contact the Estate Office, tel. Penzance 710507.

The directions for this walk are taken from Penzance. Take the A30 Penzance-Redruth road. After passing through the village of Longrock bear right for Marazion and Helston. On reaching Marazion leave the car in any of the car parks facing St Michael's Mount. A check with the tide chart is necessary for this walk as the causeway across to the island is clear only at certain states of the tide. Boats operate during the summer months but if the causeway is used it is well to remember that the tide comes in very quickly from both sides.

Assuming that the tide is low and the causeway used, walk across the beach for a short distance, joining the causeway to St Michael's Mount where convenient.

A short history of the Mount seems appropriate here. The stones now being walked on were laid by the order of Benedictine monks who were in possession of the island for 370 years. This order was known for its builders and teachers and it was these men who built the first harbour at Mousehole in 1392. In 1414 all alien monasteries were suppressed and the Mount was then granted to a group of nuns from Isleworth. In 1537 Henry VIII passed a law to regain the Mount and the property was then held by Humphrey Arundell of Lanherne until he was hanged for his uprising against the new Prayer Book. (Cornwall held to the Roman Catholic faith until the very last.) James I sold the Mount to two 'wide boys' and it then came into Bassett hands and to the St Aubyn family who are the present inhabitants, although the greater part of the Mount is administered by the National Trust. St Michael's Mount and Mont St Michel in Normandy are closely allied and St Michael himself is said to have appeared at both places.

After crossing over to the island take a good look at all the delightful little cottages facing across the harbour. Walk up the steep path to the castle and church, well cared for by the National Trust. Trading in tin was carried on here from prehistoric times and ancient writings tell us that trees surrounded the rock at one time.

Leave the island by boat or causeway and walk across the beach towards Penzance. There is a path along the top of the sea wall but,

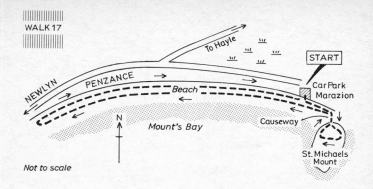

tide **permitting, the beach is the best as it avoids necessary detours**
for streams. This beach should yield some good specimens of jasper
and agate for the collector.

It is necessary, after just passing the heliport, to leave the beach
and join the footpath through the gardens alongside the main road.
It is then footpath walking into Penzance, about half a mile. A
pleasant hour can be spent here, looking around the museum, the
gardens and the Barbican. Penzance is the only Cornish resort with a
promenade although it occasionally gets torn apart during winter
gales. Time permitting, not to mention energy, walk along the
promenade past the Queen's Hotel and on into the village of Newlyn.
It is here amongst the busy fishing scene that the cormorant and
shag dive busily and the gulls scream overhead looking for an easy
meal from the fishing boats.

The walk back must necessarily be over the same ground but with
St Michael's Mount as the distant lure the way seems very short.

Walk 18

Lizard Peninsula, Penrose Woods and Loe Pool

7 miles (11 km)

OS sheet 203

The directions for this walk are taken from Helston. Approaching Helston on the A394 road from Falmouth, pass through the town following the Penzance signs. There is a one-way system. On the outskirts of the town, and half way down a hill, take a turn to the left signposted Porthleven; the cattle market and boating lake are immediately opposite. In about 200 yards a car park will be found.

Helston is an ancient market town and the home of the Furry Dance, which is said to come from a pagan festival heralding the Spring. This event takes place every year on 8 May. The dances begin at 7 am and continue throughout the day at intervals, but the midday dance is the most spectacular. The ladies wear long dresses and picture hats and the men top hats and tails. They dance in and out of the houses and shops accompanied by the local band. The town is decorated with spring flowers, particularly lily of the valley.

The walk begins close to the car park where there is a gate marking the entrance to the Penrose Woods. This estate is National Trust owned and a delight to walk through. The path is wide and firm and sheltered by trees and bushes, very suitable for a windy or wet day. The National Trust have recently provided a 'hide' overlooking the pool where one can expect to see coot, great-black-backed gulls, blackheaded gulls, terns and heron. The path wanders round the pool, passing a house on the right.

Just as the house becomes visible there is a turn to the left signposted 'Loe Bar'. Take this path, going slightly uphill. The pool is really the estuary of the river Cober whose entrance into the sea was blocked when a sand bar was thrown up during a storm in the Middle Ages causing severe flooding in Helston. There is now an underground culvert for the water to pass through but for many years the bar had to be broken manually to release the water and even today, after very severe weather, the culvert can become blocked and the town again suffers some flooding.

The path eventually emerges from the woods and out on to the coastal footpath. Mounts Bay in all its splendour lies in front and the sands beneath the cliffs stretch for about three miles. This area is remarkable for several things. It was just here that Henry Trengrouse

48

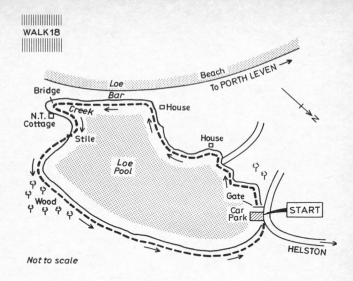

watched a ship sink and saw the drowning of hundreds of men, from
which sorry sight came his inspiration for the rocket apparatus still
used today. The bar itself is a place frequented by collectors of
pebbles and stones for they have already had the benefit here of
several weeks' polishing by the tumbling action of the sea. The
massive waves rolling in make this a dangerous place for bathing and
there are not many days of the year when the red warning flags are
not flying.

After joining the coastal path, turn left and cross the bar, which
is not a pleasant ten minutes as the going is heavy in the shingle.
This is the habitat of the sea holly and the rare horned poppy, so look
carefully for these plants.

When the trudge across the bar has been accomplished take the
path skirting the pool. This is muddy at times and uneven,
quite different from the well-kept drive on the other side. Follow the
path all the way round the pool, going inland. Cross over the stream
by a small wooden bridge, turn left, passing a National Trust holiday
home cottage on the right — a delightful spot for a get-away-from-it-
all holiday. Continue along the track past the cottage until a granite
stile in the left hand wall comes into sight. Climb over the stile and
skirt the field alongside the pool. The path goes right round the field
and into the Denbigh woods.

The walk now is easy and pretty with the woodland plants and
birds. It passes through the Loe valley and emerges through a
recreation field on to the car park.

Walk 19   Lizard Head and Kynance Cove

5 miles (8 km)

OS sheet 203

The Lizard area of Cornwall is unusual not only in its geology but in its flora, for in the district above Kynance Cove the rare Cornish Heath (Erica Vagans) can be found. The area is protected, in parts, by the Cornish Naturalists Trust and here may also be found the early purple orchid, harebells and bloody cranesbill. The pretty blue squill and the lovely thrift combine to make a pleasing picture in the Spring. As for the bird life, you can see cuckoos, ravens, a buzzard or two and kestrels while redwings and fieldfares may be observed in the winter. Snipe and mallard occasionally rest on the wet ditches. Very rarely, in winter, the short-eared owl, hen harrier and merlin may be sighted, too.

Much of Lizard village is devoted to the working of the serpentine rock for which this part of Cornwall is famous. The busy craftsmen in their workshops *cum* salerooms are usually surrounded by interested tourists. The lighthouses, ashtrays and other ornaments they produce are beautifully polished to bring out the colours of red, green and black of the serpentine.

Helston is the nearest large town and directions for this walk are taken from there. Take the A3083 road from Helston passing through the Naval Air Station of Culdrose. On reaching Lizard village a large free car park will be found in the centre of the village.

Leave the car here, walk along the road past the public toilets and, keeping right, follow the footpath sign. This path goes through a gateway and then, although this sounds improbable, the path runs along the top of a Cornish hedge. A Cornish hedge is a double stone wall filled with soil and then turfed over. Cross a field and join the metalled road leading to Kynance Cove parking area. Turn left at the road, into the car park and passing behind the shop, join the coastal footpath.

The walk goes to the left here but the Cove is such a famous beauty spot that a short walk along the path leading to the right is a 'must'. From here the energetic may like to descend the steep path to the beach, particularly if the tide is low, for then the beautifully coloured rocks will be fully exposed and the caves accessible. Refreshments may be had here during the season. *Watch the tide if crossing to the islands as it comes in very quickly here.* The detour

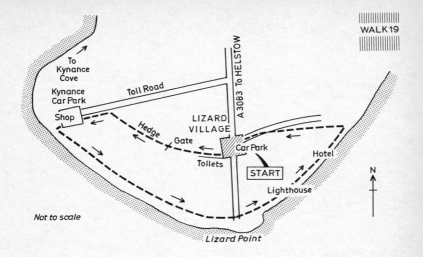

from the path down into the cove is not really necessary, however, as the view from the clifftop is spectacular and from here the shag and cormorant may be seen diving for food while the gulls scream overhead.

To continue the walk, take the path behind the shop away from the cove and follow it as it wends its way towards Lizard Point. It is wide here and walking is easy on the springy turf. On reaching the Point, where refreshments may be obtained, notice the succulent called mesembrianthemum with its big yellow or purple flowers cascading down the cliffs. The old Lizard lifeboat house still remains on the beach below the point, but it has not been used since the building of a new one at Kilcobben Cove in 1961. It is interesting to note that one-third of the world's shipping passes Lizard Point so one can see how important a lighthouse is on this dangerous rocky shore.

From this point, and for a shorter walk, follow the road back up to Lizard village. For the full walk, continue on along the coastal footpath, passing the lighthouse. It is possible to be shown around if the weather is suitable. The path now becomes steeper and narrower as it passes Bass Point and Housel Bay. The bay is renowned for its geological features such as hornblend and gneiss.

After crossing a wooden bridge the path ascends steeply. Keep right at the fork, passing in front of Housel Bay Hotel. Just past the hotel turn left, at a sign marked 'Lizard village', on to a hard track which joins a metalled road at a T junction. Turn left here and follow the road into the centre of the village, opposite the car park.

Walk 20   Kennack Sands and Cadgwith

5 miles (8 km)

OS sheet 204

This walk begins on the coastal footpath, goes inland for about two miles through a delightful hamlet and then through the village of Cadgwith and back to the coastal path for the return journey. Some of the paths can be rather muddy and there is one steep climb; otherwise the going is easy and the scenery beautiful. Part of the walk is on a Nature Trail and as this part of the Lizard is noted for its flora the botanist should be in his element. The village of Cadgwith is much used for Cornish publicity literature and when one looks down on the delightful thatched and colourwashed cottages, with the little harbour nestling in the centre, one can appreciate why.

The directions are given from Helston. Take the A3083 road from the town signposted for the Lizard. After travelling about two miles and reaching Culdrose Naval Air Station look for a turn to the left marked 'St Keverne, Mawgan and Goonhilly Downs'. Take this road, the B3293, and follow the signs for St Keverne for about five miles, passing Goonhilly Earth Satellite Station. The huge dishes spaced out on the downs are, oddly enough, side by side with ancient barrows and earthworks. In a short distance turn right, where signposted 'Kennack Sands'. Follow the signs from here for Kennack and immediately past the hotel the road goes steeply downhill towards the beach. The road is very narrow and just on the brow of the hill, on the right, is a car park. This is a free park and usually full; if so, continue on down the hill to the beach where another car park will be found on the left. A charge is made here but there are refreshment facilities and toilets available.

To begin the walk, assume that the car is left in the first car park at the top of the hill. In the top right hand corner a path leads through the gorse. In a few yards there is a fork; turn left here, along the coastal footpath. The views are fine from here, right across the sands towards distant Black Head. The rocks below are formed of bastite and serpentine and the mineral asbestos can be found.

There is soon a gap in the hedge to pass through with some iron posts to prevent access by horses or cycles. The field now to be crossed houses a caravan park. Walk through this field, then up an incline and over a somewhat awkward stile. It is rather muddy here. Next comes a steep descent and the narrow path widens out into a

52

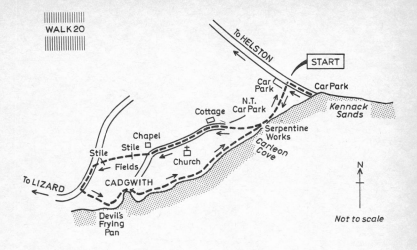

rough track. On the left, at the bottom, are some buildings. These were an old serpentine works and, although they have been to some extent preserved, it is easy to see what a considerable area they occupied at one time. There are the remains of a kiln here, too. This is where the Poltescoe river enters the sea at Carleon Cove.

Cross the wooden bridge and turn right up some steps, away from the coast. The walk goes inland now and there is a National Trust sign marked 'Poltescoe' here. Notice the bamboo and other interesting plants on the side of the path for this is part of the nature trail which continues through a lightly wooded area, past some houses, until the path widens out into a drive. Walk on and over a bridge to the road, with a National Trust car park on the right. Turn left and walk up the road, turning left at the fork opposite a cottage.

Another bridge over the Poltescoe river has now to be crossed and an interesting feature is the old boundary marking carved in the granite slab on the left of the bridge. Just halfway across will be seen a line, on one side of which is marked 'Gade' and on the other 'Ruan', for this line marks the boundary of the two parishes. A water wheel beside the river can sometimes be seen working.

Continue up the road past a cottage or two and then into the village of Ruan Minor, entering the village by the school. Turn left, past the school, and then turn right, at a sign for Cadgwith. The church is nearby and worth a visit. It was restored in 1854 but has a thirteenth century font and piscina. There are serpentine blocks in the walls and the tower is creeper-covered, making it particularly attractive in the Autumn.

Walk through the village towards Cadgwith for a short distance and look out for the Methodist chapel on the right. Leave the road here and take the path passing in front of the chapel. Cross over the field on the footpath and then climb over a granite slab stile. Notice the holy well on the left just here. Pass over another granite stile and then go downhill until the road is reached. Turn left here and follow the road to the junction.

Do not take the first road on the left signposted 'Cadgwith' but take the next road, unsigned, a few yards further on. This is a narrow lane and as it is about to wind round to the right at a sign marked 'The Lizard', leave the road and turn left. There is a sign here for the Devil's Frying Pan. Bear right through a gateway with a sign saying 'Ingleswidden'.

At the next bend keep left and in a short way look for a sign on the right for Ingleswidden. There is an open space here and some holiday cottages and at the far right corner of the open space a stile. Climb this on to the coastal footpath and almost immediately look down into the geological feature known as the Devil's Frying Pan. Take care, for the cliff is very steep here. This spectacular sight was created when the back of a giant sea cave collapsed about a century ago.

Retrace the path back to the open space and rejoin the original track. Turn right and go downhill past some cottages, indeed through the garden of one, which is the right of way. Some lovely heathers have been planted here and make a good show of colour. From here, some of the best views of the village may be had and the photographers among you should have a field day. Join the road and turn right, down the hill to the beach.

The beach is stoney and the fishing boats are drawn up close to the shore. Lobster and crab pots are stacked and nets spread out to dry and there is a shop where shell fish may be purchased. This is Cornwall at its best, quite unspoiled.

Continue on through the village and start to ascend the hill. Just round the bend is a footpath sign pointing to the right. Pass between the two rows of cottages, up the wide track overlooking the beach and at a fork keep to the right. On the headland is a small building known as a huer's hut. It is here, as at Newquay, that a huer would be stationed between August and October, watching for the shoals of pilchards which arrived in the bay during those months.

Bear to the left past the hut and keep to the coastal path, walking over Kildown Point and Enys Head. There are one or two granite step stiles to negotiate and at an open space keep to the left around the gorse bushes. It can be very muddy here in the winter. At the next fork keep to the right and then pass over another stile. Stay on the wide track nearest to the sea and then go downhill to the serpentine works again.

The walk now retraces the outward journey along the coastal footpath back to Kennack sands.

Walk 21   Helford and Manaccan

5½ miles (9 km)

OS sheet 204
Stout footwear is advisable for this walk.

The directions for this walk are given from Helston. Take the A3083 road out of the town, signposted 'The Lizard'. On reaching Culdrose Naval Air Station look out for a sign to the left marked St Keverne, Goonhilly etc. Follow this road for about one mile to a cross roads. Continue to follow the signs for St Keverne on the B3292 road. In about two miles there is a sign to the left marked 'Helford'; take this road and follow the Helford signs all the way. The lanes are very narrow and care should be taken around the sharp bends.

The car-park is situated overlooking the river. The village is closed to traffic from 31 May to 30 September — but, in fact, it is advisable to leave the car in the park at any time of the year as access to the village is very limited. The thatched cottages and local inn alongside the creek make a short detour well worthwhile.

This walk incorporates both coastal and inland paths, a 'must' for those exploring the Lizard area. It is particularly beautiful in the Spring as parts are wooded and wild flowers grow in profusion. Stout shoes or boots are necessary as parts of the woodland paths can be slippery.

Leave the car in the park and take the path clearly marked 'Coastal Footpath', near the entrance to the car park. This path follows the Helford estuary towards the sea. Daphne Du Maurier's novel *Frenchman's Creek* was written in this area and one can imagine many of its scenes when walking this path. A short walk through woodland comes out on to a tarmac lane. Turn right here and ascend the hill until a gate on the left is reached. This marks the entrance to the Bosahan Woods, a public right of way through privately owned grounds. No dogs are allowed.

The path now wends its way close to the shore in places, where numerous sea birds can be observed and the dinghies and yachts tack up and down the river. The path is clearly defined and crosses a small beach before emerging on to open fields. The view from here, reaching over Falmouth Bay, is spectacular. Walk across the first field and over a stile then turn right in the next fields, passing close by some barns, where there is a gate on to the road. Turn left and go downhill into the hamlet of St Anthony in Meneage.

Its church is worthy of more than a glance. While most of the

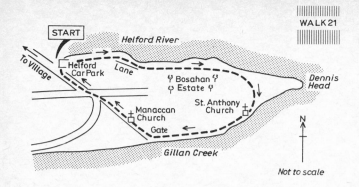

churches in the area are built from local stone, the tower of this one is built with stone from Normandy. Legend has it that, after being shipwrecked, a group of Norman sailors built the tower with stone brought from their own country as a thanksgiving for being saved from drowning on this shore. The church is still candlelit and has an ancient whipping post near the entrance.

The part of the river here is called Gillan Creek and the little harbour has numerous boats pulled up, almost on to the road.

To continue the walk follow the lane bordering the creek, inland, for about one mile. Look out for a gate on the right with a signpost 'Manaccan'. Take this path, first leading through an area notable for its unusual plants, and eventually coming to a lane at the back of Manaccan church. Pay a short visit to it and notice the fig tree growing from the walls of the tower. The altar displays some fine examples of plate made from Cornish tin.

On leaving from the front gate of the church, turn right, uphill, past the school and continue on the road, over a cross roads and downhill back to the car park. Alternatively, a field path can be taken to avoid some of the road walking. After leaving the cross roads and taking the sign for Helford, in about half a mile is a footpath sign on the left marked 'Helford village'. This goes a short distance along a wide track as if going to a farm. On reaching a gateway, turn right and follow the hedge on the left of the field to a stile. Climb this and rejoin the road not far from the car park.

Walk 22   Anthony Head

7 miles (11.5 km)

OS sheet 204

This walk, in the beautiful Roseland area of South Cornwall, offers the walker some of the most spectacular scenery in this part of the county. It offers views over the Percuil river to St Mawes and across the Carrick Roads to Pendennis Point and Falmouth and includes a coastal footpath beside the English Channel. In total, the walk is a good seven miles, with some uphill walking, but the paths are well defined and the variety offered more than compensates for the rather more than usually strenuous nature of this particular walk.

The route is given from St Austell. Take the A390 road to Truro from the town. After about five miles, look for a signpost on the left for Tregony. Take this road, the B3287, and on reaching the village of Tregony cross the bridge, bear to the right and follow the signs for Gerrans and St Mawes. This is the A3078. At the village of Trewithian, turn left for Gerrans. Pass through the village and in a short distance turn left, signposted 'Anthony Head'. Follow this narrow lane, for about one mile, driving beside the Percuil creek. Look out for a National Trust car park at Porth Farm on the right and leave the car there.

To begin the walk leave the car park and turn left along the lane you have just driven along. In about 500 yards take a track leading on to a wooden bridge. Cross the bridge and turn right, following the path alongside the creek. There is a National Trust sign directing the way to Place Manor, which is part of this walk. Cross a stile out of the first field and the path then wends its way, uphill, through a lightly wooded area. Keep to the right of the next field and, on emerging from the wood, notice a small white hut on the shore.

The views across the river here are lovely and you will see the oyster beds marked by tall sticks close to the shore. This part of the river teems with a variety of birdlife.

After passing a hut, climb a stile and at a fork in the path keep to the right. Shortly after this you will find a very conveniently placed seat. Continue to follow the path, again through a small wood until reaching the sign marking Drawlers Plantation. Go through the kissing gate here and in a short distance Place Manor comes into sight on the right. Now an hotel, it is in a perfect situation at the edge of the water and with the church spire rising behind it. Go

57

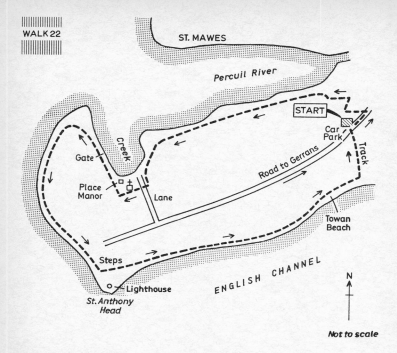

through the iron gate on to the road and turn left.

Walk up the road for a few yards until a sign for Anthony Head is reached on the right. Take this path, which goes through the churchyard where, in this peaceful spot, there is an abundance of wild flowers and hydrangeas. Turn left, just opposite the church door and, after climbing a few steps, turn right. The walk continues along a wide, although rather muddy, track until a gate is reached and a stile on the left. Climb the stile, again signposted 'Anthony Head', and go up a steep field.

At the top is a granite step stile over a wall. After negotiating this rather awkward stile, turn left and walk across the field. Continue across the open land more or less diagonally. There is a path, and after passing two coves on the right, cross over a bridge and up the other side bearing to the right. Go through a white gate and pass a small white-painted building on the right. Just here there are some steps leading on to a platform from which the view may be enjoyed. All kinds of sea birds can be seen.

Anthony Head lighthouse now lies ahead and is open to the public from 1 pm until an hour before sunset, weather permitting. Just before reaching the lighthouse ascend the steps on the left of the path. At the top, turn right, passing by National Trust holiday cottages and some toilets. There are the remains of war time buildings hereabout and the path makes its way through them. Continue to follow the coast and appreciate the magnificent scenery from the steep cliffs. The path runs near the edge in places and there are some overhangs so caution is necessary.

The coastal path from here is clearly defined and necessitates the climbing of one or two stiles. Half way across a cultivated field are some steps leading to a beach and a path running through the centre of the field. Do not be tempted to take this path but walk straight on. The sandy bay on the right is known as Porthvere.

Pass through a gap in the hedge and so on to Killegerran Head, owned by the National Trust. Go through an iron gate and past a white post and so to Towan Beach. At the track leading up from the beach, turn left and follow it up to the road. Turn left back on to the lane and the car park on the right.

Walk 23

3 miles (5 km)

OS sheet 204

Restronguet Creek

This is not really a coastal walk but one that skirts the edge of Restronguet Creek, a creek of the river Fal. It is a sheltered walk, most suitable for a blustery or damp day. There are numerous creeks on the South Coast and all provide interesting walking. Bird life includes herons, dunlin, redshank and many species of gulls. This particular creek is noted for its oyster fishing. Tall sticks, particularly visible at low tide, mark the oyster beds and the typical boats used for this industry are either working busily in the river or are to be seen anchored just off shore. The creek also boasts a most delightful inn, the 'Pandora'. Truly a fisherman's haven, its thatched roof, old beams and fireplaces offer the traveller a welcome respite. A ferry used to operate from here to the nearby Feock but now the jetty is used only for pleasure boats from Falmouth during the summer months.

The directions are taken from Truro. Leave the city by the A39 Falmouth road. At the cross roads and island at the end of the by-pass, turn left for Falmouth. Proceed along this road for several miles, passing Norway Inn on the right. Just through the village of Perranworthal the road ascends and about half way up the hill is a turn off to the left signposted 'Restronguet'. Take this road and continue along it, following the signs for Restronguet all the way. At a cross-roads turn left, still signed, into a lane going down to the Pandora Inn. The car can be left in the lane just above the inn as, strictly, the inn car park is for customers only.

After leaving the car, take the path which goes past the inn and rises slightly, passing some houses. Keep to the left at Dolphin Cottage and notice Restronguet Point on the opposite shore. Take the lower path at the next fork, passing more cottages. It is very sheltered here and fuschia hedges may be seen flowering even in November. The path winds downhill and comes out on a beach at Restronguet Weir. Should the tide be high there is a gate and a path through a field just above the beach.

The weir has now disappeared but this is a point of vehicular access to the shore. Cross the road and follow the sign marked 'Greatwood', continuing just above the creek. There is a wooden gate just after the sign and the right of way goes through this. At the

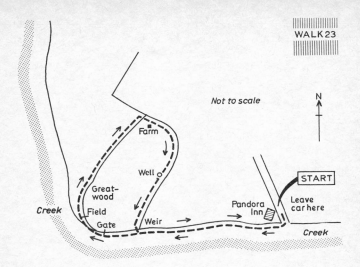

next fork take the lower path which then goes through a rather muddy field before emerging on to a tarmac road at the hamlet of Greatwood. The old manor of that name stands here, very splendid, although now hosting numerous people in a modern flat complex. Walk at the right hand side of the house, uphill, following the sign for Mylor Bridge.

Continue on the road, shortly passing a signpost for Restronguet Barton. The next mile or so is road walking, but on a pleasant, leafy lane with views of the creek on the right and offering an abundance of flora with particularly good specimens of heart's tongue fern, hard fern and wall pennywort.

At a cross roads take the sign marked 'Weir'. Walking downhill back towards the weir look for violets in the hedgerow, for they can be found here as early as January. As the road goes steeply downhill, notice two old wells on the right hand side. These, I am told, were used by the local people for keeping their clotted cream cool during hot weather. Continue on this road to the weir and rejoin the original path, turning left back to the Pandora Inn.

Walk 24

Coombe Creek and Old Kea

4 miles (6.5 km)

OS sheet 204

This walk is, strictly, not a coastal one but it affords the walker pleasant creek views and sheltered walking. The path passes beside flower fields and overlooks the river Fal. It is very necessary to wear stout boots or wellingtons during the winter as some parts are extremely muddy.

The route is taken from Truro. Take the A39 Truro-Falmouth road, turning left at the junction at the end of the by-pass. In about two miles, and half way up a hill, there is a sharp left turn signposted 'Coombe'. Take this road and follow the signs to the village. The road finishes at the creek side and the car may be left there.

Just between two cottages you will see a public footpath sign to Lower Lanner Farm. Take this path and ascend the little lane, at the top of which is a stile. Climb over and enter a field. Continue straight ahead over the top of the hill. A seat adjacent to an enclosure of trees will be found at the top and very pleasant views may be enjoyed while resting for a while.

Continue straight on, over another field where anenomes and daffodils are grown, and go through a gate and so on to a lane. Turn left here and in a few yards Lower Lanner Farm appears on the left. Almost immediately opposite on the right is a gate into a field. Go through this, again skirting a flower field, and at the other end climb over a stile on to a lane and turn right.

In about a quarter of a mile the tower of Old Kea church comes into view. Follow the road round to the right by a farm and pause at the churchyard to take a look at the eerie old tower now falling into decay. Notices warn of the dangers of falling masonry but a visit to the little chapel of ease separate from the tower is quite rewarding. The tower is fifteenth century and is all that is left of the old church. The present church of St Kea is several miles away on the other side of the main Truro-Falmouth road and is a spacious edifice built in 1895.

After passing the church continue down the lane to where it peters out and there are one or two cottages. Go through the gate on the right and cross diagonally through a field making for a gap in the hedge on the left. Step through this gap, keeping to the right and near the hedge, towards another gap where there are some farm

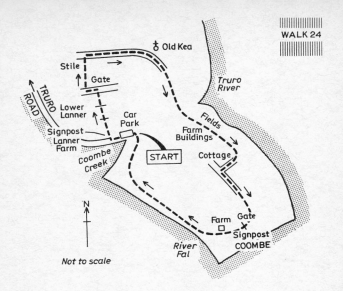

buildings on the right. Walk through the gap and on to a very muddy track. Turn right, passing close to the farm buildings, through an iron gate and continue on the track passing two cottages on the left until a lane is reached. Turn left here and after climbing a hill the road ends abruptly, continuing in a track to the left.

Walk down this track, which also can be muddy, and in a short distance, on the right, is a gate with a signpost for Coombe. Follow this sign and at the end of the short track come to a derelict farmhouse. Go round it to the left and at the back, on your right, in the corner, is a path. Take this and turn left in the field. Look out for a stile in the hedge to the left and climb over it on to the footpath. Walking is then easy and downhill back to Coombe Creek and the car.

Walk 25   Mevagissey

4 miles (6.5 km)

OS sheet 200

Mevagissey is a pretty little fishing village with winding streets, narrow steep hills, a busy harbour and interesting shops. All these play their part in making this a pleasant place to while away a happy hour before beginning the walk.

The directions are given from St Austell. At an island on the town by-pass, take the B3273 road, signposted for Mevagissey and Pentewan. The former is about five miles along this road which, as it climbs out of the valley, affords scenic views across St Austell Bay. On entering the village a large car-park will be found on the left, and this is the best place to leave the car during the season. Unfortunately it is closed during the winter, when the only car park is on the harbour. Follow the signs marked 'P' in and out of the narrow streets and eventually arrive at the harbour. There is a charge, all the year round, here as the park is owned by the harbour authority. For the purpose of this walk we will assume that the car is left here. The walk is not too long, but rather steep in places and can be muddy over the fields during the winter.

From the car park, walk back along the harbour wall past the pay kiosk and in a little while turn right, still alongside the harbour. Almost immediately bear left, up a steep incline in front of some cottages. Notice the museum beside the harbour just below the lane. Continue up some steps by the coastguard look-out and into a recreation field. Bear left across this field towards a gap in the hedge just below a row of houses. Go through the gap and along the path, which is fenced as there are landslides here. The path is well defined and after crossing over a granite step stile go down, diagonally, across a field towards the sea. There are two kissing gates here and a wooden bridge.

Cross over the bridge and keep left up a rather steep incline with lovely views across to Gribben Head with its day-mark. (A description of day-marks may be found in Walk 10.) There is a stile at the top and, in a short distance, another stile. This leads into a field where the path is not well marked — but keep to the right and, on reaching the hedge turn left, where the path is evident once again. In a few yards is a stile on the right with a view overlooking Pentewan sands.

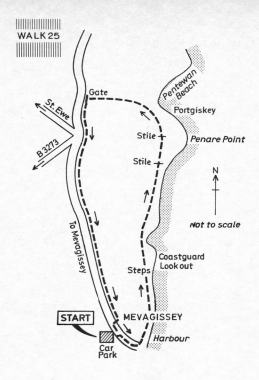

Pentewan was, at one time, a busy harbour and there is still evidence of a yacht basin and locks, and a tramway system leading out to the beach where ships were loaded with china clay and other minerals. This beach area is now completely silted up with sand and stone but many old buildings associated with the industry are still to be seen. Pentewan is a fascinating place for those interested in industrial archaeology.

After crossing the stile, walk downhill over the next field, keeping to the right, towards a stile at the bottom. On reaching this stile, where it can be very muddy in winter due to a small stream crossing the bottom of the field, climb over and keep to the right, uphill, to the top, where there is a gate on to the path beside the road. For those wishing to explore Pentewan, turn right at this point, down into the village; but for Mevagissey, turn left. The distance back by road is about 1½ miles with a footpath most of the way.

Just as a matter of interest, time permitting, do visit the little village of St Ewe. This is about four miles from Mevagissey and makes a pleasant ride. The village, which is off the beaten track and often missed by visitors, boasts a splendid old market cross adjacent to the church. The church, restored in 1881, has a screen with coving and loft of late fifteenth century work. There is a Norman font and parts of the walls show that a church of that date stood here. There is a lovely camellia tree in the churchyard, too, which is in full bloom in early February.

Walk 26   Fowey

4 miles (6.5 km)

OS sheet 200

The area near Fowey is the location for this pleasant walk. Part of
it is coastal, there is a little road walking and some field walking.
Two steep climbs have to be made along the coastal footpath but
nothing that the average walker shouldn't be able to manage with
ease. The view across the valley after entering the first field is
towards Menabilly Woods but unfortunately the house of that name
is obscured by trees. As mentioned in a previous walk, this was the
home of Daphne du Maurier and is now lived in by the Rashleigh
family again who owned the property for centuries.

Fowey itself, a delightful ancient unspoilt town, named after the
river beside which it is sited, has a deep harbour, now used by ships
exporting china clay and by yachts and pleasure craft. The
winding, hilly streets with their small shops offering the visitor all
kinds of local crafts, are a delight to browse in. The waterfront is an
interesting place, too, with boatmen ready for a chat and many
sea birds swooping among the boats. There is a museum and an
aquarium to visit as well as a beautiful old church and other
architecturally rare buildings.

The village of Polruan lies opposite, nestling into the steep cliff.
The passenger ferry plies busily back and forth between the two
places but travellers with cars must seek the Bodinnick Ferry which
crosses the river lower down.

The directions for the walk are given from St Austell. Take the
A38 Liskeard road from the town. In about three miles, just past a
garden centre on the right, turn right, signposted for Fowey. Pass
through the village of Par, turning right after passing the china
clay works at Par harbour. Follow the one-way system and Fowey
signs. On reaching a roundabout, just past a garage on the left, there
are two signs for Fowey. Take the third exit here and very soon look
out for a garage on the left called Cotswold Garage. Opposite this is a
lane, Lankelly Lane, where there is a wide piece of road leading into
the lane, and the car can be left there.

Walk down Lankelly Lane to the T junction. Turn left and when the
road peters out keep straight on along a track which can be rather
muddy. At the end of it is a gate and stile. Climb the stile into the
field and cross diagonally to the left towards the wall. Do not go

67

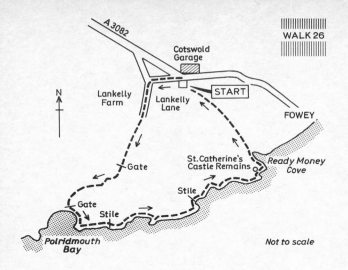

through the gate but continue alongside the wall, downhill. Now views of the Menabilly property begin. Follow the path, still downhill, as the scene opens out to give a lovely picture of the bay of Polridmouth with a house and pool just above the beach.

Continue to the bottom of the hill, through a gate, and turn left away from the house. The path now ascends through National Trust land into the Lankelly Woods. Climb a stile at the top of the hill and turn right, following the path round the edge of the field on the sea side. This is now the coastal footpath and easy to follow, with a few steep ups and downs, across a wooden bridge and into Coombe Haven, a delightful sheltered cove. The views along this stretch of coast are across the channel; Polperro in the far distance and the nearby Polruan visible most of the way.

The path eventually passes through an area known as Day Fields which were given to the people of the town of Fowey by Mr and Mrs Allday in 1951. Go through the kissing gate into the woods and keep straight on. Ignore the paths running off to right and left and follow the wide track to the junction. Turn left here—but at this point a detour can be made.

Instead of turning left, turn right and the path will lead into St Catherine's Castle, a fortification built by Henry VIII for defensive purposes. Notice a block house on either side of the river just below the castle. From these two towers a chain was suspended across the river in days when Fowey was subjected to much sacking from pirates. When this danger seemed imminent the chain was raised, thus preventing access into the estuary. Gun emplacements and cannon are still within the castle walls but, apart from its historical

68

interest, the place offers the best vantage point for views down the river and of both Fowey and Polruan. It is a favourite spot for photographers.

To return to the walk. After turning left, down the track, bear right at the bottom and on to a road above Readymoney Beach, so-called because of the underwater artifacts beached here when divers have been exploring the many wrecks in this area. Pass by the pretty cottages and follow the road, uphill, bearing to the right. Almost at the top of the hill, on the left and opposite a pair of iron gates a track goes uphill. Take this track and continue walking for about half a mile until it ends at a lodge and gate.

Through this gate, and I expect rather to your surprise, will be the car!

Walk 27   Polkerris and Polridmouth

5 miles (8 km)

OS sheet 200

A great deal of mud may be encountered on this walk.

Directions for this walk are given from St Austell. Leave the town by the A390, Liskeard road. After about three miles and just past a garden centre on the right is a sign for Fowey. Take this road, the A3082, which goes through the village of Par, where English China Clays have their own port for the shipping of their product. Take the signs for Fowey, which go round the one-way system. In about 1½ miles, and almost at the top of a steep hill, is a sign, on the right, for Menabilly and Polkerris. Take this road and in a very short time go round a sharp right turn for Polkerris. A steep, narrow hill leads down into the village and it is necessary to leave the car about half way down on the right where there is a car park.

This walk is in Daphne du Maurier country, very close to the lovely house of Menabilly where she lived for a number of years. Polkerris is a delightful little village nestling among the steep cliffs. Lush vegetation, quaint cottages, an old kiln and fish cellars; Polkerris has it all. The initial ascent from the village is steep and can be slippery and the walk back can be muddy in places.

Assuming that you have been on to the beach, walk a little way back past the cottages and turn right on to the coastal footpath. Pass the toilets and continue to follow the path, uphill, through the woods— a picture in Springtime with primroses and bluebells. On reaching the field at the top, turn right and after a few yards climb over a stile. A view now opens out to show the expanse of St Austell Bay. The evidence of the china clay industry may seem rather jarring but it is essential to the economy of the country as well as to Cornwall and is a small price to pay for the wealth it brings from natural resources. One quickly forgets the Port of Par by looking ahead at the sweep of the coastline towards Mevagissey.

The path is easy to follow over the fields. It is recommended to take a sharp left turn uphill in the third field and then across the top and over a rather difficult stile on to Gribben Head. There are signposts to 'The Gribben' but the day-mark on the headland is as good a landmark as one could wish (A description of day-marks may be found in Walk 10.) Take a look at this tall monument, erected as a guide for shipping during the 1800s. Look eastwards from here and notice Polruan in the distance. Further on is the coastline beyond

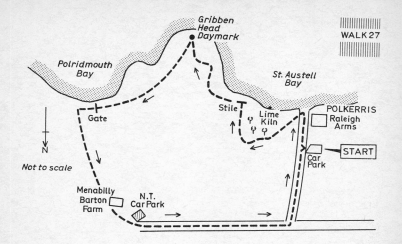

Polperro.

Follow the path away from the day mark going downhill and round the little beach at the bottom. When the sign marked 'Polridmouth Beach' is reached, take the left hand path up the field away from the coast. However, before doing this, make a short detour by continuing along the coast path for a few yards. As it bends to the left a house set almost on the beach comes into view; the lake beside it and the cliff ahead give it one of the most picturesque settings possible.

Back to the footpath — walk uphill through the field until it joins a track. This is where it can be very muddy. Passing a farm on the left and into another field keep to the farm track and through a gate on to a lane which leads back to join the road down into Polkerris again.

Just after joining the lane you will see the house of Menabilly to the right. The estate is now in the care of the Rashleigh family who owned the property for generations and now live in the house again.

Walk 28   Cheesewring, Bodmin Moor

3 miles (5 km)

OS sheet 201

This is one of the three moorland walks included in the book, and the archaeological and geographical interest provided makes it one of the best short walks in the Bodmin Moor area. The terrain is a little rough in places and some climbing has to be done to the top of the tor.

The directions are given from Liskeard. Take the Callington sign from the town centre on the A390 road. In a few hundred yards turn left at the sign for St Cleer. On reaching this village and just before the church turn right, going downhill. Almost at the foot of the hill and on the right is a very fine example of a holy well, the structure of which was rebuilt during Victorian times. The well is dedicated to St Cleer and an ancient Cornish cross also stands within the well enclosure.

Continue on down the hill until the T junction is reached, then turn left and follow the signs for Minions, turning right at the T junction on the moor. There is also a sign for the Hurlers here. Just before the village, on the left, is a parking space and a sign for the Hurlers pointing along a rough track. Leave the car and start the walk along this track.

The stone circles on the right of the track are soon reached and a Department of the Environment notice gives a brief description of their date and possible use. This part of the moor abounds with evidence of very early habitation followed by the quarrying and mining activities of later dates. The engine houses, now mellowed and often surprisingly beautiful, are dominated by Cheesewring, or Stowes Hill (1249 feet), with its south slope scarred by the Cheesewring quarry, last worked in the 1950s. There are numerous paths leading to the Cheesewring which is so-called because of its structure of flat rocks of granite, naturally formed, piled one upon another. Those at the base are smaller than those at the top and the overall appearance is of a vast mushroom 24 feet high. The views from here, extending over both Devon and Cornwall, are truly magnificent.

An interesting place to look out for, before the final climb to the top, is a cave-like structure with some engraved granite blocks around it. The name 'D. Gumb' is carved on one. Mr Gumb, his wife and 13 children are said to have lived in a cave here. He was a

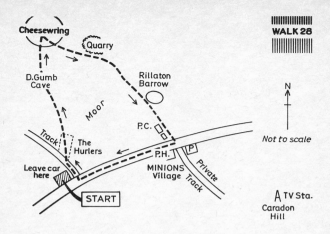

Cheesewring

Quarry

D.Gumb
Cave

Rillaton
Barrow

Moor

N

P.C.

Not to scale

Track

The
Hurlers

P.H.

P

Leave car
here

MINIONS
Village

Private

Track

START

A TV Sta.
Caradon
Hill

mathematician and astronomer and markings on other rocks show evidence of his pursuit of these subjects.

Descend from the hill and keep to the path around the fenced edge of the quarry. On reaching a wide track—which was the tramway track into the quarry at one time—turn right. Just past some fenced mine shafts, bear right, diagonally, across the moor towards a barrow, distinctive on the highest point of that area. The detour is well worth while as this is the Rillaton Barrow in which the famous corrugated gold cup of that name, dating from 1500 BC and now in the British Museum, was found. One can see a short distance into the barrow through the gap around the entrance stone.

From here, walk back to rejoin the track, turn right and follow it to where it joins the road. Turn right and make your way into Minions village, where there is a shop and an inn—and your car.

Walk 29

Bodmin Moor, Brown Willy and Rough Tor

4½ miles (6.75 km)

OS sheet 200

Choose a clear day, without a strong wind, for this walk.

This is rather a tough moorland walk which includes climbing the two highest tors in Cornwall. It is advisable to choose a clear day, for the mist comes down quickly in the high places; a very windy day should be avoided, too.

The first tor to be climbed is Rough Tor which is owned by the National Trust and is the site of a memorial to the Wessex Regiment, 1,311 feet above sea level. There are numerous hut circles on the lower slopes of this tor and an old clapper bridge spans the stream crossing the approach track. The second is Brown Willy, 1,375 feet above sea level and giving views across the moorland to the A30 road at Jamaica Inn and Dartmoor to the North. Much can, and indeed has, been written about Bodmin Moor. All of it makes interesting reading but it is sufficient for me to say that this walk is a useful initiation into hill walking and, while it is not too long, it *is* rather strenuous.

The directions are taken from Camelford, an interesting old market town. Leave it by the A39, travelling north. In a very short distance, half way up a hill, take a turn to the right marked 'Rough Tor'. This road, which is very narrow, is signposted all the way out to the moor and you will find a car park where the road ends and the moors begin.

After leaving the car, walk down to the stream and the clapper bridge crossing it. Notice the Stannon china clay works on the right, owned by English China Clay Company. Cross the bridge and follow the track up the slope ahead. It is shorter in distance to approach the summit by bearing to the right and ascending the second half at the steepest angle, but for the easier, if longer, route I suggest that the track up the grassy slope be followed, to the left of the tor.

On reaching the top of the lower slope, turn right and walk across to the massive boulders perched one above the other on the peak. This is not absolutely necessary but I feel that having come so far it is rewarding to complete the climb to the top where the Wessex Regiment memorial may be seen. The rocks are granite and are part of the intrusion of igneous rocks rising through the slates from Dartmoor out to the Isles of Scilly. This is a site much favoured by geological study groups as well as by climbing parties.

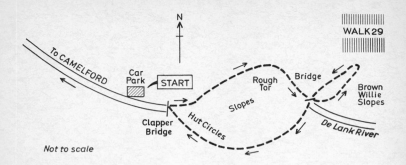

After pausing for a while to take in the view and pick out various landmarks, walk down the other side of the tor, keeping to the left. There are boulders to contend with but it is easy enough to pick a way through. Brown Willy rises ahead and it is necessary to cross the De Lank river between the two tors. You will see a bridge in the valley and a gate through the fence. Cross the bridge, where it is rather muddy at most times of the year, and start the climb, which is gentle to begin with, up Brown Willy.

Follow the track, well defined, leaving a shepherd's derelict cottage on the right, where moorland ponies are often found sheltering between the two ridges. As the track bends away to the left, leave it and make your own way — there are numerous paths — up to the summit. The last few feet up to the cairn and trig point are steep. Here the wind blows, whatever the weather, and it would be inadvisable to climb this high in a howling gale. The mist comes down quickly, too, so do choose a good clear day for this trip. The moors stretch ahead and traffic can be seen moving along the A30 at Jamaica Inn in the distance. In the marsh below rises the river Fowey. This area is known as the Fowey Downs.

For the return, descend from Brown Willy by the most convenient route, and make for the bridge again. Cross over this but do not climb over Rough Tor. Instead, turn left alongside a wall for a short distance then strike diagonally across the lower slopes towards the foot of the tor. It is uncomfortable to walk too close to the base as it is so rocky. Keep bearing to the right, round the hill, and when the car park comes into sight again look out for the prehistoric hut circles which can be clearly seen, particularly when the grass is short. Join up with the original track and cross the clapper bridge again into the car park.

An interesting monument is to be found in the field on the left of the bridge, a memorial to Charlotte Dymond, a local girl, who is said to have been murdered on this spot. One can get,to it but the ground is always boggy.

Walk 30 Madron Moor

4 miles (6.5 km)

OS sheet 203

Madron Moor is one of the granite outcrops running down the centre of Cornwall and out under the sea to the Isles of Scilly. It is from the contact with the country rock of slate that the mineralization occurred. There is, as a result, evidence of extensive tin mining in this area. Compared with Dartmoor, or even Bodmin Moor, Madron is comparatively small in size but it is rich in archaeological remains. Here we find the greatest number of ancient burial grounds, old crosses, stone circles and standing stones. The burial sites range from barrows of Bronze Age origin to Megalithic Quoits, which are massive stones standing upright with a covering capstone although they were originally covered with soil.

An unusual monument, known as the 'Men an Tol' (Cornish for 'Stone with a Hole') consists of two upright stones separated by one with a hole through the middle. Stone circles are classed as Megalithic monuments and, as the name suggests, are a circle of any number of rough-hewn up-standing stones. The purpose of these circles is obscure but the general belief that they were used for religious or ceremonial purposes is the most likely one. Standing stones, seen all over the county, are usually placed as way-marks and in some cases (as in the one on this moor) as memorial stones to a chieftain. Men Scryfa, Cornish for the 'Stone with Writing', can be seen during this walk.

The directions for the walk are given from Penzance. Leave the town by the B3312 road for Madron village. This is off the A30 just before the Heliport. Follow the signs for Madron. The road goes through the village. Continue on up the hill until reaching a sign post on a sharp left hand bend for Ding Dong Mine. Follow this sign and, where the lane deteriorates into a track, leave the car. The view across Mounts Bay and St Michael's Mount from this point is quite lovely.

Take the rough track ahead until an engine house to the left can be seen, marking the site of the old Ding Dong Mine, famous for its production of tin and copper in the past. Leaving this and continuing on the main track, bear right. Do not take the first path leading across the moor on the left but take the second one after a few more yards. There are no signposts and the tracks wander

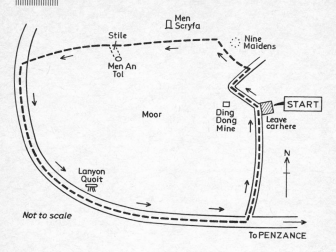

through the heather.

Pass through a wall where there is a wide gap. After about 100 yards a stone circle can be seen on the right although a few of the stones have collapsed. There is a great feeling of mystery about this site. It may be rather muddy here but the paths are well defined and the puddles can be avoided. Keep to the left after passing the circle and go downhill; Men Scryfa should be visible from this point to the right at the bottom of the hill and can act as a landmark. Pass a derelict cottage nearby in which it is interesting to note the massive lintel over the fireplace.

Continue on up the cart track and pay a visit to Men Scryfa in the field on the right. Return to the track and in about 100 yards come to a signpost in the left hand hedge marked 'Men an Tol'. Climb the stile here and, in a short distance, the Men an Tol comes into view. Legend has it that if you can pass through the hole without touching the sides you will be cured of back troubles. As late as the nineteenth century children were taken to this site and passed through the hole, in the belief that this would cure them of rickets.

Leaving the Men an Tol in its isolation, return to the track and turn left. The track continues until it meets the road. At this point turn left and continue walking, passing Lanyon Quoit on the left after about half a mile. The road eventually reaches the signpost to Ding Dong Mine again and the lane leading back to the car.